To
DR. MANGINO,
WITH LOVE AND GRATITUDE
FOR ALL THAT YOU'VE
DONE FOR ME.

Anita

Gimme
Shelter

Deno Seder

Gimme
Shelter

HOMELESSNESS AND THE EFFORTS TO END IT

DENO SEDER
ANITA SEMJEN

π
PHILOS PRESS LLC
WASHINGTON, DC

CONTENTS

*"Oh, a storm is threatening
My very life today.
If I don't get some shelter
Oh yeah, I'm gonna fade away."*

"Gimme Shelter"
The Rolling Stones

INTRODUCTION

A family of geese marching with graceful aplomb crossed the narrow road leading to the men's emergency homeless shelter in Rockville, Maryland. It was my first night as a volunteer back-to-work mentor.

From the outside, the shelter looks like a large, typical, fairly new suburban home – stately porch columns, sixteen windows, manicured lawn. Inside, it is a temporary home for two hundred men.

In the vestibule were a dozen or so men, forlorn and isolated from the main shelter. I would learn later that there were no available beds for these men and that at nine o'clock each night a bus would take them to an overflow shelter. It was a freezing February night, and I was relieved to see that no one was turned away.

A large man, who I learned later had been a federal prison guard, approached me and asked if he could help me. I said, "I'm Deno Seder and I'm a new volunteer." He told me to sign in and go to the Voc Lab.

The shelter's Voc Lab was a large room with eight computer stations. My job was to help the men use the computers to find job listings on the internet. In some cases, my job was to help them learn how to use a computer or learn how to get Medicaid or legal help or emergency medical care or temporary housing. I would often just talk with the men, get to know them, listen to their problems and try to be helpful and show some empathy.

Many of the men were educated and had work experience. Others had drug and alcohol issues, physical and mental health issues, felony convictions or issues I knew nothing about. Some had a stark antipathy toward me and my efforts to help them. A few had aggressive tendencies.

During my four years as a volunteer, some of the more difficult moments came when I would try to help someone and he wouldn't let me.

But the best moments came when a guy would walk into the Voc Lab and joyfully, proudly announce that he got a job. Smiles and high fives all around. Sometimes a big hug and tears.

The interviews in this book are with people who have experienced homelessness and with people who are working to end it. The interviews have been edited for clarity and brevity.

When it comes to homelessness, George Leventhal knows what he's talking about. As an elected official in Montgomery County, Maryland, he was an advocate for the homeless. He wrote his doctoral dissertation on the subject. He speaks to the public about homelessness. And he is unequivocal and passionate in his advocacy. When we interviewed Dr. Leventhal for this book, he told us, "The climate that is set by elected leaders and the appropriations that are provided by legislative bodies are the biggest determinants of whether we can place more people in housing." He also gave us a history lesson in, among other things, how systemic racism has contributed to homelessness in America.

Jennifer Speight has a Ph.D. in survival. As a single mom in her twenties, she developed pancreatic cancer, became overwhelmed with medical debt, got addicted to drugs and experienced homelessness for three years. Today, she is represented by the Community Family Life Speakers' Bureau in Washington, D.C. and speaks publicly on topics such as health inequities in communities of color, inner city youth development, mental health and wellness issues.

For Tecoy Bailey-Wade, childhood trauma and abuse led to PTSD, an addiction to crack cocaine and alcohol, fifteen years of life on the streets and seven years in a federal penitentiary. After her release from prison, Tecoy found people and programs to help her move forward with her life. Tecoy is now helping others who have experienced homelessness. She is the Housing Manger and Resident Coordinator at Open Arms Housing in Washington, D.C.

His performance as Gloucester in a film version of King Lear got rave reviews. But after a series of bad breaks, deteriorating health and an eviction, Jim Zidar found himself in a homeless shelter. "It was like being in a Kafka novel. It was an absolute nightmare," he remarked during the interview. Jim has since found permanent housing.

Gordon Brown told us that it can cost over $100,000 a year to sustain a person in homelessness (e.g. policing, emergency rooms) but less than $25,000 to house that person and provide services and employment opportunities. Gordon is the of founder of A Place to Stand, a nonprofit providing services to people experiencing homelessness in Fairfax, Virginia.

It was a remarkable accomplishment -- the end of homelessness for veterans in Montgomery County, Maryland. Lynn Rose, the Community Engagement Specialist at the Montgomery County (MD) Coalition for the Homeless, described it for us: "We started with a subpopulation of people experiencing homelessness. We found every single veteran who was homeless and found homes for them all. That takes a lot of resources, a lot of coordination. And then we rallied our networks, our community support, our different organizations. That's how we did it for veterans."

His artwork reflects a mysterious and sophisticated semiotic quality. It is intricate and engaging. Clifton Thompson told us that he uses aesthetic elements found in African woodcarvings to produce stunning three-dimensional effects. But it was difficult to create art in a homeless shelter, where he was forced to go after quitting his job as a trucker because of health issues. Clifton is now in permanent housing and creating new works of art.

For those working to end homelessness, helping others can be gratifying. Ashley McSwain is Executive Director for Community Family Life Services in Washington, D.C. She shared this reflection with us: "There have been a lot of moments where clients come back and want you to know how well they've done, or they come back and share with you how something you said made all the difference to them. I've got lots of stories like that."

Being a homeless trans woman has its own challenges. Here is how Grimaldi-Francesca Sanchez describes it: "Some of the women might be placed at a male shelter where that presents another challenge, or the women's shelter where the women may not want them, so that presents another whole challenge." Grimaldi-Francesca is a transgender woman who has experienced homelessness and is dedicated to advocating for equity and equality for women and trans people of color.

For his doctoral dissertation, Aaron Howe is conducting an ethnography of homeless encampments in the District of Columbia. He is the co-founder of Remora House, which provides supplies and assistance to individuals living in homeless camps and shelters in the D.C. area. When asked how we can make people more aware of homelessness, Aaron said, "We need to change the discourse around street homelessness away from criminalization or clean up or harassment to one of a humane solution, to actually funding services that we know work."

Andre Wyche is a polyglot who speaks five languages with varying degrees of fluency. He has a degree in accounting, worked in the tech sector, was a public school teacher and served in the Air Force where he experienced combat operations seven times. Suffering from PTSD, Andre became homeless. He is now married and living in permanent housing.

The psychological trauma of homelessness is real. Denis Elis, an Army veteran and computer scientist, described it this way: "My life just made a complete stop. You kind of get lost. There's no direction. You don't know what's going on and what's going to happen. I know it's going to be different for everyone because everyone's situation is different, but I kind of chose to be homeless to save myself. I was contemplating killing myself because my mental health was degrading so badly." Today, Denis is working and living in permanent housing.

Marlene Aiyejinmi is a survivor of homelessness, incarceration and addiction. "Being on the street, I got robbed a lot. I got raped a lot. I didn't care if I lived or died." Marlene spent eight years in prison and credits her time there to getting sober, setting life goals for herself and adjusting to a new way of thinking and living. Through Community Family Life Services Speakers Bureau in Washington, D.C. she shares her life experiences with women who look to her for hope and inspiration.

Homelessness has a deleterious effect on children. Wanda Steptoe, Executive Director of New Endeavors by Women located in Washington, D.C., offered this explanation: "A lot of times with children who are experiencing homelessness, they have a tough time in school because their parents may not know how to provide the support that they need to be successful. So in our family program, we have a teacher who works three evenings a week to help them. The teacher provides tutoring, supervised homework assistance, extra help in math and reading. And that's our goal, to help kids be successful and to understand what education can afford them as they become adults."

Will Gundlach served in the U.S. Army Psychological Operations (PSYOP) to persuade and influence foreign populations in support of U.S. military objectives. As the youngest cyber security expert in the Army, he supervised 60,000 people and oversaw the construction of schools, roads, bridges, canals and other major infrastructure projects. But his experience in the military did not translate to the kind of experience domestic employers were looking for. Consequently, Will became homeless, sleeping in his car for three years. He now has his own apartment and speaks publicly on behalf of homeless veterans.

A failed business and health issues forced Heather Thomas-Wyche into homelessness. "But thankfully, our family was considered the fortunate homeless. Even though we lost everything, we went straight from where we were into a transitional housing program. So we didn't have to stay in a shelter, we didn't have to stay in a motel, and we didn't have to stay in our car." Today, Heather is Fairfax County, Virginia's Head Start Policy Council Vice-Chair where she advocates for homeless and low-income families.

The purpose and scope of this book are to educate people about the reality of homelessness and to encourage individuals, charitable organizations, local, state and federal governments to create more programs and funding to ultimately end homelessness in America.

GEORGE LEVENTHAL, Ph.D.

George Leventhal is Director of Community Health at Kaiser Permanente. For sixteen years, he served as a Montgomery County, MD Councilmember. He was Senior Federal Relations Officer at the Association of American Universities and Legislative Director for U.S. Senator Barbara A. Mikulski.

George holds a B.A. degree in English from Berkeley, a Master's degree in Public Administration from Johns Hopkins, and a Ph.D. in Public Policy from the University of Maryland.

He has been an active advocate for ending homelessness and wrote his doctoral dissertation on the subject.

Hi Dr. Leventhal. Good to see you again. I understand you're at Kaiser Permanente.

Yes, I'm Director of Community Health.

I see where the company is investing several million dollars to address homelessness in the region.

Yes, we gave away $2.4 million in the region last year.

And they've pledged $36 million nationally.

Yes, it's a major philanthropic priority for the company.

Why does the company do that? What's in it for them?

Kaiser Permanente was the United States first managed care health organization. So for the first time, I believe it was in the 1940s, you paid a monthly fee and subscribed and then all of the medical services were covered under your monthly fee. Since it's not a fee for service program, the bottom line is improved.

When you're healthy, if you utilize the system less, but we still collect your premiums, that's a better deal than if you're sick and you're a heavy utilizer, because we don't charge fees for service. There are some healthcare systems that incentivize multiple visits and the argument is that managed care is better because it's in the interest of the system to address all of the determinants of health.

So not only do we want to see you when you're sick, but we want to give you advice on how to stop smoking, how to lose weight. And then more broadly, the companies became more sophisticated about this as the decades have gone by, addressing the social determinants of health, because only twenty percent of your health status relates to the visits with a doctor or within the four walls of a healthcare entity. And the rest is due to lifestyle and environmental issues and broad societal issues. So being housed, for example, to get to the topic we're discussing, makes a very big difference for your health. There's research that shows that life expectancy for a person experiencing homelessness over a long period of time is thirty years less than housed individuals on average.

So broadly, the company started to understand that its own bottom line was improved and also its commitment to social health and social welfare, which was there from the beginning. It's always been a company that cares about social health and addressing broad social determinants of health. It is the mission of the company. After two and a half years, I've met the top leadership who believe in social justice. They believe in addressing housing stability and economic opportunity and all of the things that we work on.

And also, in addition, not-for-profit hospitals and health systems, the Internal Revenue Service requires an annual report showing that at least three percent of gross revenues goes to community benefit, broadly defined.

So pretty much every not-for-profit hospital or health system will have a community health department or a community benefit department or people who work in philanthropy and community development to promote social good and try to quantify that in order to report to the IRS, "Here's the amount that we contribute to community benefit." So for all those reasons, I have a job.

What is your impression of the last administration's position on homelessness compared to Biden's?

The largest chunk of my career has been as an elected official, running for office every four years. And I fully understand that the political climate is going to make more difference than anything else. So as I was completing and defending my dissertation, Trump was elected and took office. And it was clear that the idiots in his administration didn't care about poor people and were not going to stay with the Housing First philosophy and indeed, the whole cast of characters in the administration were people who were either oblivious or actively hostile to the Housing First effort. Now, Joe Biden is president and suddenly we've got a lot more federal money in the pipeline and more coming.

So the climate that is set by elected leaders and the appropriations that are provided by legislative bodies are the biggest determinants of whether we can place more people in housing. I'm more optimistic under the Biden administration. Communities want to and should adopt evidence-based best practices, and you need hefty appropriations. And so if we get hefty appropriations, I think there's a methodology in place that has in the past and can again in the future lead to a downward slope in the rate of homelessness. We had a significant downward slope during the Obama administration, and then it ticked up again under the Trump administration, and I'm optimistic that under the Biden administration, we'll see more progress.

When did you first become interested in the issue of homelessness?

I was on a county council and I was Chairman of the Health and Human Services Committee, so I oversaw the emergency housing and rental subsidy programs. A good friend of mine pitched me on the concept of the 100,000 Homes campaign and said, "Look, if you really want to bring an end to homelessness, this is the methodology that's going to get you there." And I flew out to Orange County and Community Solutions was doing what they called a boot camp, training for local government and local Continuum of Care. And I got swept up in the rhetoric and the persuasive efforts to enlist in the campaign.

And then in 2015, here in Montgomery County, we did in fact get to zero homelessness among veterans, which was our near-term goal. So it was proof of product that if you apply these methodologies, you can actually identify a particular subpopulation and get to zero, as we did for veterans in Montgomery County. That confirmed my interest in the topic and my awareness of the different methodologies which I had already been researching for my Ph.D.

What have you learned about how people become homeless?

Well, there's a multiplicity of issues and the individual circumstances are different. I mean, fundamentally, people become homeless because they can't pay the rent or the mortgage, but you're mostly talking about a rental population. So that's the number one issue -- can't pay the rent, lose your housing, you're on the street. But there are things that contribute to all of those, I mean, poverty, right? Employability, mental and behavioral health, those are all contributing factors. But the number one issue is, can't pay the rent.

Are you familiar with My Digital Data Locker?

Absolutely. We're very involved with that. We're heavily promoting it. We were a major philanthropic contributor to its development. We're super excited about it. It's being piloted in two cities, Baltimore, and New York, and we contributed $150,000 to Baltimore to develop it. It's a software platform that enables anybody to upload their vital documents into the cloud. So it's particularly relevant to homeless people, because people experiencing homelessness are always at risk of losing their stuff. You park it somewhere temporarily, you lose it, it gets stolen, you get evicted, they toss it on the street, you lose your stuff. And your stuff could include your birth certificate, your social security card, it could include all of the indicators that prove you're you. And you need those things in order to get Medicaid, you need it in order to get a Housing Choice Voucher, you need it to open a bank account.

So this enables folks very easily to keep track of their documents and to provide them to government officials or bank tellers or whoever you need to share your documents with. You can just get them on your smartphone, and it's portable and it's very easy. So it's a new application and we're very excited to have been one of the philanthropic supporters and I expect to be moderating a panel about it at the American Public Health Association this fall. We're trying to lift it up as an example of an exciting initiative in public health and social policy.

If you're doing any Zoom lectures, or anything like that, please put me on your list.

Sure. We're going to be hosting a Regional Forum on homelessness probably in the month of June. And there will be a presentation about the Digital Data Locker there. So we'll get you on the email list for that and you're welcome to listen in.

Thank you. I was on a MCCH (Montgomery County Coalition for the Homeless) Zoom conference the other

day and one of their PowerPoint charts indicated that
Black people make up sixty-four percent of people in
our homeless system, but sixteen percent of our
Montgomery County community. What are the historic
and current reasons for that, and what can we do to
address it?

Well, I'll give you another statistic – sixty percent of
White families in Montgomery County are
homeowners while only twenty percent of Black
families are homeowners. So interestingly enough,
tonight I'm lecturing on the topic, The Racist History
of Single-Family Zoning, because it's a very timely
issue around the United States and in Montgomery
County. State and local governments are looking at
the relationship between single-family zoning, which
says that in order to live in most of the developed land
area, you have to be able to purchase and own one
home on one lot, no townhouses, no apartment
buildings, no duplexes, no triplexes, no fourplexes.
They're all illegal in most of the residential land in
Montgomery County and in many other places.

And the history is very clearly racist. There's just
no question that when the Supreme Court in 1917
passed the Buchanan decision that said a local
government may not in law segregate. A local
government may not by law, say, "Black folks can't live
here." The crafty communities around the country
found ways around that by creating economic
segregation, and single-family zoning was around the
same timeframe. Communities started to say, "Okay,
fine, we're not allowed to say Black folks can't live
here, but we are allowed to say you can't have any
apartment buildings here." And the Supreme Court
agreed to that in the Euclid decision, which is why all
of zoning is known as Euclidean zoning.

Why is it called "Euclidean?"

It's not because of the Greek father of geometry, even though zoning is a geometric exercise. It's because of the town of Euclid, Ohio, which imposed a ban on industrial uses on their main street and the owner of that land challenged that and said, "Well, that's illegal. We want to build what we want to build," and the town elders said, "No, no, no, we want stately homes and a grand boulevard." And of course that had racial implications. And the lower court ruled for the real estate company and against the town, saying that it was a violation of Buchanan, saying that it had a discriminatory and racist effect. But the Supreme Court overruled that.

And that was in 1921 and ever since we've had Euclidean zoning, which has become the basis for the entire planning profession in the United States, which is founded upon racist principles and continues to use terms like compatibility and neighborhood character which are so much a part of planning principles that you completely forget how racist they are. So neighborhoods are supposed to be a certain way, and they're supposed to have a certain look. And that's exclusionary, because you can only have homeowners and you can't even have duplexes. So you have to have a certain amount of means to buy into a segregated neighborhood.

There's three major tools that had racist effects in the housing market throughout the 20th and into the 21st century. Exclusionary zoning, which I've just spoken to, was one. The second was racially restrictive covenants, which the Supreme Court upheld. So even though the Supreme Court said in 1917, that a town could not designate Black areas and White areas, the Supreme Court later ruled that between private parties, it was okay for you to say, in the deed to your property, "This property may not be sold to a Black person." There were artful ways of describing the racial covenants. I'm lecturing on this tonight. One of them said, "This property may not be sold to a member of any race whose death rate is higher than the White race."

So it was an artful way of saying that you can't sell this property to a Black person. Okay, so you have exclusionary zoning, you have racially restrictive covenants, and then the third leg of the racist stool that created generations of disparity in wealth and in homeownership is redlining. Both through official federal policy in the 1930s under Roosevelt, and well into the early 1950s under Truman, the federal government as a matter of policy would not provide FHA backed or GI Bill backed mortgages to Black people. They would only make them available to White people. And they did it through what is called redlining, by identifying parts of the city that they wouldn't invest in. Those, of course, were the Black neighborhoods. And that's called redlining. So those three de facto and de jure policies created this massive disparity in who owned homes.

When the GIs came home, a lot of them bought homes with GI Bill and FHA backing. But those were the White families. So that's the late '40s and early '50s. So what does that mean? They build equity in their homes, then in the 1960s, their children inherit all that wealth, they buy homes, that increases the disparity. So that even though the Fair Housing Act was passed in 1968, the Fair Housing Act said on its face, you may not discriminate, but it said if you have a bigger bank book, you can buy a property in this neighborhood. But it didn't provide an opportunity for folks with a smaller bank book to move into that neighborhood. And single-family zoning explicitly prevents that because the barrier to entry is too high.

And then, of course, that relates to where kids go to school, right? Where you live, determines whether you get to attend Walt Whitman high school or Paint Branch High School, and all the implications of that for college admissions and professional opportunities.

So this is structural racism. There are structures in place, that, again, I'm repeating this statistic 60% of homeowners in Montgomery County families are White, 20% of homeowners are Black. So you see this in our affluent County, where you have affluent Black people but still there's so much to catch up on.

The net worth of White families in the United States is ten times the net worth of Black families in the United States. Structural racism creates these vast wealth disparities. So it's harder for Black folks to obtain housing, it's harder for them to hang on to housing. There are many other causes, but it's all related to structural racism, and there you are.

Can I build a tiny home on my lot in Montgomery County and make it available to a low-income family or homeless individuals?

You can now because the county liberalized the Accessory Dwelling Unit Law. Until just recently, you couldn't, but now you can. But it's still heavily regulated. You have to apply to the county and get a permit and you have to conform to certain rules, like you have to live in the main house. You can't put an adjacent property or an accessory apartment that's not already there in an investment property. So it's still restrictive.

You've probably heard the FDR quote, "The test of our progress is not whether we add more to the abundance of those who have much, it is whether we provide enough for those who have too little." Have we regressed from that philosophy?

Speaking of FDR, when I talked about redlining and how it was official federal policy under FDR and under Truman, is that news to you or are you familiar with that?

It is news to me.

So I want you to look up two pieces of reading material. I'm actually going to share my screen with you since we're on Zoom. segregatedbydesign.com. It's only 18-minutes long. It's a video that describes the history of redlining and you should watch it. And then there's a book by Richard Rothstein called *The Color of Law*, and you should read that.

So President Roosevelt articulated these noble aims, and you're asking if we've gone backwards since the New Deal. But in fact, the New Deal in many ways discriminated against Black folks. Many of the benefits available under the New Deal, including housing subsidies and many others were not available to Black people. So the New Deal, from the perspective of an activist government that tries to solve problems, had much to commend it, but it was a creature of the 1930s and the 1930s were a very racist time in the United States. And Roosevelt was dependent upon a coalition of Northern liberals and Southern racists in order to get anything through Congress. So he couldn't vigorously and actively take on Jim Crow and segregation because he would lose his majority in Congress. And that was the great compromise. In order to advance these socially progressive goals, they basically could only benefit White people, otherwise you couldn't have gotten them through the Congress, especially through the Senate.

The art of compromise as they say.

Yeah.

We were talking about tiny homes in Montgomery County. I was looking at Seattle, Portland and some other cities. They look like they have a pretty good track record in setting up these tiny home communities. What's your impression and thoughts on the tiny home communities?

Well, tiny home communities are illegal in Montgomery County. Single-family zoning does not allow them. They are, in effect as defined by law, mobile home parks. Each tiny home moves on a trailer It's just a little fancier looking than your traditional mobile homes. And there are no mobile home parks under the zoning code in Montgomery County. I think tiny homes are an option. I mean, you need tons of policy options to address the diverse needs of people experiencing homelessness. A homeless family can't live comfortably in a tiny home, but a single individual potentially could, so it depends on the needs of the client.

Some of the ones I saw were permanent. They were not on trailers. They're actually permanent.

I've seen a lot of them. There's a nice tiny home settlement called The Boneyard, not far from my house in Northeast D.C, just east of North Capitol Street. So if you want to see some attractive, tiny homes, just Google, The Boneyard, D.C. And you can call and make an appointment and visit. It's something to see.

During your campaign for County Executive, ending homelessness was one of your themes. How did that go over with voters?

I think one of the things I learned is that, people appreciate it when you dedicate your public career to meeting the needs of the less fortunate, but they don't vote for that. That's not what voters in Montgomery County are looking for. Voters in Montgomery County are heavily skewed towards White homeowners and they're interested in preserving their style of life and their quality of life. I mean, this dialogue that we're having about single-family zoning, it would be radically unpopular among most voters. And I was pretty unpopular by the end of my career and I did mostly work on affordable housing, homelessness, access to health care for the uninsured. These were all things that I worked on as an elected official, and people thanked me for it. But then they told me on multiple occasions, "I so appreciate the work you've done in the HHS arena, but I'm voting for somebody else."

Yeah, property values.

Which is an issue. I've discussed this with Nan Roman, the head of the National Alliance on Homelessness. Homelessness doesn't poll. It's not on voters minds. When you ask voters, "What's the number one thing you care about?" Homelessness isn't even in the top ten. And so it hasn't been lifted up as a major political priority, because the voters are housed. And they don't see it as a need for them. It's not an issue.

And so in order to make it a political priority and the appropriations that it would take, you need to have political momentum. And let's hope President Biden does. I mean, he's making substantial investments.

And let's hope those continue. I do believe it's a solvable problem, but it takes money, and appropriating money means you have to have the political will.

George, thank you for your time and your expert comments.

My pleasure. Thank you, Deno, thank you for your interest in this topic. Let me just close with this. As we survey the great public policy challenges that we face as a society, and there are many, climate change certainly is one, obviously COVID-19 is front of mind for everybody. I find homelessness to be as compelling a public policy challenge as any other and the reason being very simple -- acuity of need, people suffering in abject misery with nothing, sleeping in their car, in the woods, just abject misery before our eyes. And there is no other subpopulation I can think of whose suffering is clearly greater. There are sub-populations of suffering and a range of suffering, but it would be hard to identify any subpopulation that is suffering worse than people experiencing homelessness.

And by virtue of that, you would think that homelessness ought to be a top public policy priority. And it's a manageable problem. I mean, there are 1.2 million homeless people, something like that, depending on how you count it and how you estimate it. Millions and millions of homes turnover every year. Can't we identify a subsidy structure and a new construction structure and a way of housing these folks? How difficult could it be? But you have to have political will and you have to have the appropriations.

And certainly there's a tradition in Montgomery County and elsewhere in the faith community stepping up to this challenge, but the faith community can't marshal the resources that the government can. And bottom line is, federal, state and local governments have to lift this up and make it a budgetary priority.

You've given me a wealth of information.

Great. I enjoyed the conversation.

Take care.

You too.

(The following excerpts are from the doctoral dissertation, "The Stubborn Persistence of Homelessness" by George L. Leventhal)

"Even though more than 1,000 communities adopted 10-year plans to 'end homelessness' in the first two decades of the Twenty-first Century, and hundreds of communities adopted aggressive implementation strategies to that end, no community in the United States achieved that goal. Moreover, as this dissertation argues, convincing demonstration of the efficacy of policy intervention has proved elusive, as has a clear consensus among advocates regarding the best path for future intervention.

"Despite well-intentioned efforts, an actual end to veteran and chronic homelessness remains a distant goal... The most decisive factor in the decline in veteran and chronic homelessness between 2007 and 2016 was the availability of federal housing vouchers, especially VASH vouchers.

"It is very difficult for homelessness researchers to separate their personal commitment to the issue from a need to analyze objectively efforts to address it. As an elected official in Montgomery County, Maryland (County Councilmember from December, 2002 to the present), the author of this dissertation was an active participant and believer in the recent efforts to address homelessness, including implementation of the Housing First philosophy, development of a 10-year plan to end homelessness, participation in the 100,000 Homes Campaign, Zero: 2016 and a successful effort to house every identified homeless veteran in Montgomery County.

"There is an inherent conflict between advocacy and objectivity. With an ongoing effort underway to house homeless clients using public resources, believers in the effort may be reticent to publicize information suggesting goals are not being met, because disseminating unsatisfactory results could diminish support for the effort. Hence, a disconnect exists between advocacy for ending homelessness and the analytics necessary to document whether progress toward that goal is being achieved.

"Without admitting that previous goals have not been met, the Obama administration's Opening Doors plan (2010) conceded that 'We believe it is important to set goals – even if aspirational – for true progress to be made.'

"Setting 'aspirational' goals is the job of advocates. Analyzing whether those goals are met is critical to evaluation. It should be asked whether researchers in the field can overcome their own advocacy biases to analyze why widely-adopted methodologies are not ending homelessness. Even the name of the most respected information clearing house for homelessness research, the National Alliance to End Homelessness (NAEH), suggests the bias that leads researchers into the field: the organization's title offers the presumption that homelessness can be ended. The alliance is an advocacy organization first and a research organization second, as is true for many other organizations in the field. While Culhane and others have suggested that 'ending homelessness' is merely a 'slogan,' actually ending chronic and veteran homelessness has been a significant policy focus and it is important to ask whether explicit promises to achieve that goal have been kept. It is also important to ask whether any ongoing social problem can actually be solved outright, or only managed.

"There is reason to hope that homelessness, particularly among chronically homeless clients and veterans, will continue substantially to diminish. Nevertheless, the problem stubbornly persists, especially in large cities with a major media presence that influences public perception, such as Los Angeles, New York and Washington, D.C."

JENNIFER SPEIGHT

Jennifer Speight experienced a period of homelessness as the result of medical debt accrued while battling cancer. She shares her experience advocating for an end to the stigma surrounding homelessness and for improved healthcare access for all people.

Jennifer led community organization efforts on behalf of homeless shelters and has spoken before the D.C. City Council about the needs of people experiencing homelessness. She stays connected to the communities she serves and through the Community Family Life Services Speakers Bureau speaks publicly on issues such as health inequities in communities of color, inner city youth development, mental health and wellness, and building strong families by providing tools to help keep them strong. Jennifer also works as a professional narrator for TV and radio commercials, films and videos.

Why don't we start with your background? Where were you born and raised?

I was born in Allentown, Pennsylvania, but I grew up in Virginia for the most part. My dad is military, Coast Guard. I have two other sisters and a brother, so we grew up mainly in the Stafford, Virginia area where we did elementary and high school.

And then once I graduated high school, I moved to D.C. I never really got a chance to fully enroll in college. Every time I did, something happened, some type of traumatic event, like me being pregnant, although not really a traumatic event, but it was definitely life-changing. And so that would be the first big thing, and the second would be my diagnosis of cancer, which just stopped part of my world for the most part, because I was still working. But then I wasn't able to work.

How old were you when you were first diagnosed?

I was diagnosed at twenty-seven.

What was your reaction to being diagnosed at that early stage in your life?

I don't really think I had any emotion at that point when it came to the actual moment of diagnosis. It wasn't even really a diagnosis just because what it took to get there.

What did it take to get there?

First, it was just written off as food poisoning. Then I kept on going back to the emergency room. I went back about four times in less than a month and at one point, it got to, "We're not giving you any more pain medicine," and my first thought was, I didn't ask for any prescriptions. And then it was like you're seeing the wrong kind of doctor. And I had just found out I was pregnant again after I had my daughter. What I thought was food poisoning was actually hyperemesis, which is just really bad morning sickness, which is what I experienced earlier during my pregnancy with my daughter. I was high risk and lost about forty-five pounds throughout the whole pregnancy, but I was still working full-time.

So I didn't know that that was not normal. You know what I mean? I was told that the symptoms were in my head, that what I was experiencing wasn't true because they couldn't confirm anything with the tests that they ran. I believed it for two seconds just because I was tired. I was depleted of energy. I was constantly vomiting. I normalized a lot of things just because I think culturally, that's just what we do as Black women.

I went back to the hospital one last time, and I didn't get any attention. I didn't get what I felt like I needed. I was being dismissed. I got angry. Real angry. I got beyond angry. I was enraged. I was almost beyond hysterical at that point, not even crying, just with anger, and they wanted to dismiss me to give time and attention to somebody else who was probably just trying to beat a cold. I felt like I was being treated like I was a problem, like I was an issue, and the reason why I say that is because around this time, it was high in the season for the homeless to come into the emergency rooms to seek shelter and warmth and get something to eat and freshen up for a little bit and that was I guess the routine that this particular emergency room had been experiencing.

Was that here in Washington, D.C.?

28

Yes, it was here in Washington, D.C., and I said, "If you want me to leave, call the police. I'll leave in handcuffs. But I'm not going home. You cannot make me leave," and I think they heard me. I know they heard me. The security guard was the same security guard I saw the three or four times I went there before, and I looked at him, and said, "I'm not going home. Call the police. Call my doctor. That's all I want you to do. Call my doctor. Have my doctor tell me to go home. But I'm not going home if you don't call my doctor." And I threatened to sue and some other stuff and they put me in the back room.

I don't know how I was able to take a nap, but I was woken up by the doctor and he said, "We found something that piqued our interest. Do we have your permission to take a further look at it?" I stood up on both feet and I was like, "I knew it. I freaking knew it. This is about to get real now," and I didn't know what to expect. So I just waited and was determined to educate myself about the process I would be going through. I knew something was wrong, and then I learned about the pancreas.

And had you not reacted that way and advocated for yourself in that way, what do you think would have happened to you?

I literally had no time to waste. If I would have waited even six more months, it would have been beyond stage three, beyond stage four. My liver was failing. My kidneys were failing. I was jaundiced. I wasn't having any bowel movement. By the time diagnosis came, I was just, I didn't even tell my family.

Why didn't you tell them?

I think it was just a way of me protecting all of us. I know that out of the obligation of love, they would have wanted and felt compelled to do something, but I didn't know what they were supposed to do and I know they're going to be looking at me for the roadmap, and I'm trying to see the highway before I can build the roadmap. So my thought process was, well, if I need something, I'll ask, but I didn't want them to have to restructure their lives for me. I had a child. I had my own place. I didn't want to be dependent.

But also, I couldn't afford to exert any extra energy and I was afraid that my family was going to just do too much. At the end of the day, they were going to stress themselves out. They're going to worry me. At that point, I wasn't eating every day, but I was still functional. I was still okay. But once that cancer word gets thrown in there, everything changes. Either way, I didn't know what was going to come of it. I wanted to be okay and that was just my way being okay.

I'm curious about this phenomenon of knowing that there's something in your body that's not right in spite of all the doctors' expert opinions.

What the doctors were saying was that whatever I had, it was benign. There's probably nothing there. You're fine. If there is something there, it'll go away just like everybody else experiencing it.

Did they do tests and take scans?

Yeah, pictures. Did the white blood cell counts. There was nothing that gave any type of awareness that I had stage three pancreatic cancer, nothing other than I didn't have any bowel movements and I wasn't able to sleep. I wasn't able to eat properly. Those things, but to them, that wasn't a symptom of the physical. That was symptomatic of the psychological.

With the nurses, I found talking to them really helped. I asked how attentive their doctor really was. How should I attack this? I did that just more and more with whatever I encountered.

I knew how I felt. Even if there's nothing there, something is still wrong. You guys have to figure it out. That's what you're supposed to do. I'm here because I'm supposed to be here. You have to be your own best advocate.

I didn't feel like they saw me as an advocate. I was agitated. I was angry to them. I was unreasonable to them because of my temper, but why can't I just be passionate about wanting to live? Why can't I just be passionate about not wanting to die, about not wanting to go home to my two-year-old and not waking up? I was definitely afraid that that was going to happen to me and I don't know how I got the angst, the energy. I don't know what fueled me to stand there and deal with all the trauma.

Do you think the medical profession spends too much time treating the symptom and not the patient?

If we give more individually humanized treatment, we can treat both patient and symptoms pretty easily, but there's no real platform for that. I think the medical profession does not leave room for medical ethics in the sense of just humanizing it. It doesn't have to be textbook. Medical professionals are taught a different type of ethics minus the humanization. At the end of the day, everyone has their own unique experiences. I was told that what I was experiencing was in my head. He said that because I was a single, unwed, Black mother, living on the edge below the poverty line.

Women are fighting the same struggle on different levels. And I would like to see them coming together in the same space, not knowing each other's stories, but being able to feel that connection in the room and just work off of that. I would love to see something like that happen because of this book. I would love that, because I felt super alone and I was always questioning, "Am I right? Am I doing the right thing?"

I felt like if I would have left the hospital with a prescription for how to eat right, with a proper dietitian and a nutritionist, I wouldn't have had to fight opioids for two years and stay on that cycle of addiction.

Where did you have the surgery?

It was George Washington University hospital. And I did go and get a second opinion, but it was the same. I just took into consideration the actual hospital itself. It's a university hospital. I figured, "Okay, there's going to be a lot of forward-thinking people there. I should be able to get somebody to listen." But they're not built for that. They're not built to listen. They're programmed to objectively look at things and get a quick turnaround, and I feel like that takes all of the empathy out of medicine. I don't know if sterile is the right word, but you don't feel confident that this is going to be the place where someone listens to you.

You think going to the emergency room would be an emergency, but you're sitting there waiting, and four hours later, you still haven't been triaged. Finally, at five and a half hours, you're being triaged but you still have to wait for another three hours. So for those people that say, "Well, why haven't you gone to the emergency room sooner?" It's not that I didn't want to go. It's the whole bill processing factor and babysitter for my daughter because obviously I can't take her.

Also, I wasn't quite at a point where I felt like I needed the emergency room.

I was also pregnant during this time, but I was not able to keep the baby. I would have had a son, but I had to make a decision to terminate the pregnancy so I could get the tumor removed. He would be going on eight in August. For me, that was the worst part of it all. So it's just me and my daughter to this day.

I had two emergency surgeries before I had my tumor removed, one of which was my appendix that ruptured from all the convulsing and being dehydrated. I didn't even tell my family I was pregnant because I didn't want them to have to feel that loss. About a year later, I finally told my mom.

Did you have anybody that you were talking to, a therapist or social worker?

No, I did not. Again, going through something like this, I didn't have a patient navigator. I didn't have anyone or anything to help navigate, like this is your checklist before surgery, right? I just had my doctors and I knew that I could correct what they were telling me in the sense of making it more relatable to me and what I'm going through now, but that's as far as I got. A lot of the wants and needs of me recognizing that came after the surgery when I was in the hospital on bed rest because I was intubated for the first week. I was still conscious and fighting an infection. If after that week I still needed help to repair my kidneys or liver, I was going to be in trouble. So I'm listening to everybody telling me everything, but I can't really respond, and I wasn't sure if I was going to have to be put on a transplant list just from what they were saying.

Everything happened rather fast. I believe it was six or seven months from diagnosis to surgery, and it was prolonged a week because my daughter's grandmother passed away in a house fire.

Oh my god.

Yeah, I had my surgery the day of her services. I eventually did have my breakdown. I wasn't able to hold everything together. I had my breakdown in the hospital. They took the ventilation tube out of me and I kept on seeing house fires, just these babies and families dying in house fires, and that was so triggering and I just cracked. I just cracked, but I'm glad I did because that was a way for me to be able to mourn her and then mourn the loss of love and family. Did I make the right decision? I knew I had to stay focused for my daughter. It was just a lot. So I did eventually let it seep in.

When you do your public speaking, do you talk about your medical experience?

I do. I'm actually very comfortable with it. I speak publicly about my particular health experience and how that correlates to society with inequitable healthcare for women of color. So yes, I have been speaking on that. Most recently, I've been speaking out on homelessness and moderating seminars and events versus actually being a panelist. I like tying in the conversation with the service providers, the lived experiences and taking questions from the audience.

You look healthy. How are you feeling these days?

I feel like in parts, I'm still recovering. Physically, I don't have any broken bones or any open sores or wounds, but mentally and internally, I'm still struggling with a lot. I have hernias, which at times feel like my stomach is being ripped open. I have times where I just pass out. I get syncope episodes. I've been to cardiologists and a neurologist. At one point, I thought I was having seizures along with passing out just because of how I would come out or come to, but I feel like going back to get help for all of this is still triggering my past experiences. I don't know if I'm seizing. I'm not biting my tongue, but my body is stiff as a board. My memory is off. When I left the hospital, they gave me fentanyl and morphine. I knew I didn't feel the best sometimes, but I felt this was supposed to help with my pain. I got addicted. And then I instinctively saw how people judged you, especially if you were homeless. Now, if I'm going through pain, I won't take pain medicine. I'll meditate. I'll drink tea. I'll do yoga. I'll go to sleep. I'll take a shower.

At the end of the day, medicine is here to help, not hurt, and I found more hurt in medicine than help. I found more help in community with people like you that want to build platforms and create these moments and structures to give people not just the voice but the leverage for the voice to be heard with the book or with video. I think it's really important for it not to just be here with us, but I think it's super important that this should be in the classrooms. This should be like Medicine 101, right? Leading with empathy. The more stories that are shared, I realize that I'm not alone. But why is this such a thing that needs to be corrected? Why hasn't it been corrected way before?

The way people look at the homeless bothers me. Even when my daughter and I see homeless people with the camps and stuff, we humanize it. I remember being with a friend and she was like, "Oh, look at those dirty homeless people," and I'm like, "No, no, no. We don't do that, especially in front of my daughter. Those are people that either need help or can't get the help that they need." We don't do that because we were there before and she thanked me for checking her and humanizing it in a way. That's often people's perception of what homelessness is and who it affects. It just really boggles my mind. It's just super sad.

People think the homeless want to be homeless, or they're homeless because they're drug addicts. These people think they're omniscient and they know why people wind up being homeless, but the truth is, people have health issues and they lose their jobs. They get evicted. I heard that story so many times and they didn't choose to be homeless. That was the last thing they wanted.

Where were you living and when did you first experience homelessness?

We were living in a co-op apartment for over twelve years. Never had any issues, but for the last ten months, I wasn't able to pay my rent, and I was very open and honest with the office. But I eventually got evicted. I think the landlady waited for as long as she could to start proceedings, but I eventually got evicted, and I couldn't get any help.

Where did you go to try and get help?

The main office at Virginia Williams [Virginia Williams Family Resource Center]. That's where everything is processed for homeless families. Sometimes you had to wait five or six hours. I remember going down there and very regularly bringing my food stamp card with me and helping women buy their kids snacks because they didn't have any money. I had to go there more than once and I didn't really understand the women's anger when I first started going down, but after experiencing the services offered to prevent homelessness, I just found it really ironic how institutionalized the process is. I mean, you walk through a metal detector. You can't have food or water. You can't be on your phone. You have to sit down. There's armed security inside. They're monitoring everything you do. If they don't like how you're talking, you have to leave. It was almost like being sentenced before a trial.

At the time, I honestly did not think we were going to be homeless. But then we became homeless, and I didn't think we would be homeless for more than six months. We were homeless for over three years.

I had my daughter with me by my side with everything I did. I gave myself moments to be sad but not for too long. I could cry, but I couldn't break down.

Was the homeless shelter in D.C.?

Yes, it was here in D.C.. It was actually a D.C. General Family Shelter, which D.C. General was the hospital campus. It sits on the Anacostia River. Beautiful landscape when you're looking the other direction. But on the campus, it has the D.C. jail.

On the other side of the shelter, you have an inpatient treatment facility for psychiatric care and for drug treatment, both directly behind the main building, and then you have the old morgue, which was no longer in use, but it was just a super creepy building that hoarded rats and other creatures of the night. And then you had a smaller access building or run-off shelter behind the main building that sat right next to the inpatient psychiatric treatment facility.

Can you describe life at the shelter?

At any given time, you would see people outside, incapacitated, selling drugs, human feces at the bus stop, which would be the main bus stop in front of the shelter, broken glass everywhere, and then you'd have kids playing just two, three feet outside of that.

There were bed bug outbreaks, mice running through the building, raccoons and possums in the ceiling. I was just amazed at how this is what $100 million looks like. The community partnership which operates Virginia Williams operates with over $100 million dollars to prevent homelessness and provide services and we deserve better. And along with that, we organized for a laundry facility to be put on site, to be built on site. You would have families that had to take the bus, sometimes three buses with all of their children and two bags of clothes across town to a laundry facility and then have to come back, but then get in trouble because they missed curfew.

So very early on, I recognized that this was not going to be us. I was going to do everything in my power to change everything and I had to be very strategic about it. So every morning, I got up and got dressed like I was going to work and people just assumed I worked in the shelter. I never corrected them, but I always operated in a way where I asked leading questions, questions that required answers. Not everybody would ask certain things. You wouldn't expect homeless persons to ask certain things of management or why certain processes are executed and expect to get an answer. Well I demanded answers. I would get information and give it to my case manager because I didn't know I wasn't supposed to, but I operated not like a normal homeless client from what I was told. I wasn't getting any help from my case manager, and I told her, "This is how we're going to operate."

How did your case manager react to that?

I was just so amazed at how okay my case manager was with it, but I'm like, "Look, this is the information I got. This is what I did. Give this to your people so they can give it to their homeless clients." That's how it started out, and then I started organizing within the shelter and that's what put the spotlight on me.

How many women and children in the shelter?

There were over two hundred families in the main building. It was more children than women in the shelter, and that was super triggering because, I mean, these kids were angry. They were angry. They were sad. Their emotions were all over the place.

That was my next question. How did this experience affect the children?

They would get in trouble and so I asked for more programs for children. So we got more play time. We got more hours. Then there was a team room built and little things were helping but that still wasn't enough. We were still getting moldy food. We were still forced to take cold showers because the hot water was turned off at eight o'clock. We're still subjected to curfews even though most families were working. I saw families in there. I didn't see felons or criminals or addicts. I saw working families. I saw mothers that wanted the best for their children. I saw daughters there with their fathers. I saw families and I demanded to be treated as such. We started with the help of a non-profit, Washington Interfaith Network, and started organizing. I was one of the main ones in shelter and there were a lot of other great people that helped, and it became just a better facility and better services.

Do you remember your first night at the shelter?

It was horrible. My daughter was choking on dried cereal and I'm yelling and screaming for help, but they would not come past the threshold. My daughter's choking, but I could not get help to come into my room, and it took a minute for it to connect. "Okay, Jennifer, take her outside in the hallway and get help."

When you say "threshold," do you mean they couldn't come in the room?

Yes. Protocol and procedure. I'm expecting somebody just to come to the rescue but I had to take her outside the hallway and still no one touched her. All over protocol and procedure. I tried to put my finger down her throat. She vomited, but she was still choking. So I was able to get her to take some water down and that's what helped, I guess, dislodged, but yeah, I think that's what really woke me up in the sense that this is not a safe space.

I read that you had worked at the State Department. Did you have any savings or a pension from working there?

No pension, but luckily, I had my 401k and that was my retirement. I depleted that and took the penalty just to help keep us afloat, but that just wasn't enough. By the time those funds ran out, we had already been evicted, and we were well on to our way to homelessness.

Before your own experience, what was your perception of homelessness?

I didn't have any real experience other than what was given to me on TV, and then I didn't see any White homeless people. Most of the homeless people that I saw, they were Black men or Black women, right? Or prostitutes or something like that. I didn't see homeless children.

I always say just because you're housed doesn't mean that you're whole. I wouldn't say my experience in homelessness was traumatic. We weren't mugged or robbed or anything like that. It was just a really bad experience for anybody who experiences homelessness. I just became more knowledgeable about what's really out there. I think it was important just to share that knowledge. And I had to deal with NIMBYism, Not In My Backyard.

How do you deal with people who think that way?

A group was formed here to keep the newer emergency family housing units outside of the good neighborhoods because they were afraid of criminals and drug activity and crime rates going up and robberies. I would go to some meetings, neighborhood meetings. A lot of them were standing room only, but I remember at one particular meeting for, I think it was either Ward One or Ward Three. I just remember really being able to connect with the opposition on what they want for their families. Everybody wants their family to be happy and safe. That's it. Everybody wants their home to be safe, and I agreed with them. I'm a single mom. It's just me and my daughter. I don't want to move to a neighborhood that I'm fearful of. I was able to remind them that we both agree on wanting the same thing, and that I'm not a murderer. I'm not a drug dealer. I am homeless and I would be one of your neighbors one day in this emergency housing unit.

What kind of reaction did you get?

I mean, the chairs shifted and turned. I got apologies after that, dinner invites. Let's sit down and get some wine and talk. I can't fault people for their fears, but if your fear is misplaced because of prejudgments, then we have to fix that, right?

With homelessness, there are so many prejudgments. With addiction, there are so many prejudgments and unwillingness to be receptive to the human side of it. But if I hadn't gone through any of this, I don't know if my perceptions would have changed so easily and so fluidly. So my experience helped me see the light.

How can we incorporate the topic of homelessness in our political dialogue?

Well I don't think it would be a hard thing to do at all. Everyone supports mental health and wellness, but isn't that a part of homelessness? Everyone's for boosting the economy, but isn't that part of homelessness? Education for the kids, but doesn't that affect homelessness? So for me, we should treat homelessness as a clinical issue and as a wholesome issue and as a political issue. As I've said, just because you're housed doesn't mean you're whole. Just because you're employed doesn't mean you're whole. Just because you're going to therapy doesn't mean you're whole. There are a lot of other things that affect homelessness and how a person or a family got there. Homelessness is most often not by choice.

I see a lot of forward progressive thinking, but it's not done seamlessly across the board. I think if we take what's happening in California and other places, they're utilizing what we already have. They're taking containers and making homes out of them. That's genius. Why would that not be across the board?

Homelessness is a worldwide issue. It is an international issue. Housing cost is an international issue and now with COVID, it's definitely an international issue. It just amazes me how with all the politics and all these forward-thinking people, all these philanthropists, all of these voices with power, and no one's speaking up about it on a seamless platform, no one is speaking up about homelessness.

I believe that homelessness is a symptom, but some people think that just providing housing is a cure and don't realize that housing alone is not a cure. It can often produce nothing but more symptoms from anxiety, from depression, the fear of losing everything that you just received, not knowing how to sustain or hold on to it. Moving forward, what does next year look like? Will I still be employed? Am I employable? Are people going to like me where I get employed? It's just this never ending cycle of anxieties. It's a crazy monster and often going from homelessness to being housed can exacerbate that, and if there aren't proper services put in place prior to help strengthen that resolve of being connected to your home, then a lot of people will fall back into homelessness. They've been housed, but then they fall back into homelessness or they've been helped in a way where you would think from the outside looking in that homelessness would not be the option, but then a year or two later, they're back into homelessness. I completely blame the system. It's not the people.

Jennifer, I could talk to you for another hour because this has been a real a learning experience for me. You're confirming some thoughts and suspicions I've had and you're opening up my mind to new ideas and approaches. I'm confident that by sharing your story with others it'll open their minds as well. Thank you so much for taking the time to talk with me.

Thank you, Deno. This has been an awesome experience. Thank you so much for choosing to interview me and I look forward to hearing from you.

Take care Jennifer.

Peace.

TECOY BAILEY-WADE

Tecoy Bailey-Wade experienced homelessness for a long period of time. Today, she is the Housing Manager and Resident Coordinator at Open Arms Housing in Washington, D.C. She monitors progress in attaining daily living goals, conducts apartment inspections, tracks annual progress of program participants, provides housing stabilization services and offers counseling and crisis intervention services.

Tecoy is currently pursuing a bachelor's degree in social work from the University of the District of Columbia and plans to work toward a master's in social welfare.

Tecoy, you're at Open Arms Housing right now, correct?

Yes, sir, I work for a nonprofit organization.

And you're the housing manager and resident coordinator?

Yes.

Tell me about that. What do you do in that position?

I initially applied for this job coming out of transitional housing at New Endeavors By Women. Back in 2010, I had just come home from the penal system and I applied for this job and was called in for an interview. The job initially was a certified peer specialist. I understood what a certified peer specialist was and I wanted to give back because of all the hurdles and trauma that I had gone through and how I overcame them and that sort of thing. So I had a desire to share with other women that they could overcome their trauma. They're not unique. Other people have had the same experiences. I just wanted to share the hope.

So I applied for the job and they hired me as a certified peer specialist and a year later, they had me full-time as a housing manager/residential coordinator. I wear several hats at the organization.

I've built a rapport with the majority of the women in that facility. At the present time, we serve twenty women. It's a site-based program and my duties are to organize groups, allow them to pick the topics, have game days with them, prepare special meals and that sort of thing, to bring in a sense of family because a lot of the ladies here at the facility suffered with a lot of trauma. It is mental health, substance abuse, a mixture of so many different traumas and I could relate to all of them.

And I didn't have to, but I chose to be transparent with the ladies. I just had to put myself in their position, which I had been in before, sharing my interpersonal stuff with people I didn't know. I was hesitant at first, but I became an advocate of that.

So my role at Open Arms, I pretty much did groups. I did game day to kind of break the monotony with the ladies so they wouldn't think it was always about groups and talking about how they felt. Then I began to have a rapport with the ladies. I pretty much knew their behavior patterns and when they would act out. I would be the segue to kind of get them to understand that it's okay. It's okay to express your feelings but we're actually here to help you. I had that rapport with them that would kind of level the playing field. So it became kind of easier for them as well as for myself to move forward.

And then on the housing management side, I had to put on a different hat because my responsibilities at the organization are to work with vendors, work with D.C. Housing Authority, do leases, do inspections, make sure the properties are up to par with the D.C. code. And I have to give out letters when you're late for your rent or you miss your payment of rent. I collect rent and that sort of thing. So I have to kind of wear two different hats. On the residential coordinator side, I'm the good cop, but on the property management side, I'm the bad cop, if that makes any sense. Working with women who come from the environment that I came from, it can be challenging to reach them.

Can we talk about the environment you came from and the trauma you experienced?

We can. Early on as a child, I suffered with a lot of abandonment issues. I suffered with a lot of sexual abuse, a lot of dysfunction in my household growing up. I was kind of like passed along and I never understood why I wasn't with my real parents. My father's sister raised me and it was very strict in that household. I'm really sharing some stuff with you.

Let me say, if you're uncomfortable with anything, you don't need to...

No, I'm okay. I'm pretty comfortable with it because my past experience makes me who I am today. I'm clear on that. The sexual abuse, I was afraid to talk about it for a lot of years. I felt like nobody would believe me, and when I finally told it, I had actually moved in with my mom by then.

The sexual abuse started when I was like eleven or twelve. And for so long, I was afraid to tell anyone, and when I did tell, it was like nobody believed me, or I was being blamed like it was my fault. I went to Rape Crisis Center and I know that it's something I have healed from even though it took me down a road of self-destruction for so many years, so many years.

I took off to the races looking for love in all the wrong places and street life. That's where that led me. On top of that, I didn't realize that I had a post traumatic stress disorder and I didn't have a safe place to talk about how I felt. The way I was raised, it was like you stay in a child's place and certain things were just swept under the rug and it led me down a path of destruction, self-destruction.

I became homeless. There were things going on in my adult life where I just couldn't go home anymore and so I hung out in the street, living from pillar to post. I did that for, oh my goodness, I want to say almost fifteen years of my life. I was caught up in that vicious cycle and it was all stemming from internal conflict because of the trauma that I had experienced and didn't address.

It wasn't a good feeling. I went to different mental health providers but I didn't stay. They diagnosed me with PTSD. I started taking the medication, then stopped. I told them that all I needed was therapy, somebody to talk to.

I became caught up in a lot of drugs -- crack cocaine, marijuana, alcohol, which led to promiscuous behavior and some other activities that landed me in a federal penitentiary for seven and a half years.

While I was incarcerated, I had a lot of time to do some soul searching because I had kids that I wasn't a mother to. My family had to raise them. When my mom died, they became separated and a whole host of other things happened because of the traumatic experience I was going through.

While incarcerated, I went to different trainings. They had this program called RSAT, which was a substance abuse program. I went there and became educated on that. I took a lot of self-help trainings and after doing the seven and a half years, I had realized that I had missed out on so much in life. I felt shame and guilt, but it actually wasn't my fault. It wasn't your fault, Tecoy, that you had abandonment issues. You were sexually abused by your biological father. You were in a household where you really couldn't talk about things as a child. You were an only child. You had no brothers, no sisters. And at the age of sixteen, you were having kids of your own.

And then after your release, where did you go?

Upon my release I came to New Endeavors By Women and there were several staff members who really, really, really saw a lot of potential in me that I didn't think I had. I didn't think I had it, but they saw different. I had nowhere to go. I could've gone different places but I knew I would have ended up in the same environment that I suffered from, so I didn't want to make that decision.

I started over and being in New Endeavors By Women gave me a lot of confidence to just move forward with my life and try something different. They convinced me that I had a lot of potential that I didn't think I had. I had all these dreams as a child that actually became reality. It became reality. I moved forward and a lot of people helped me in that facility and I'm so grateful for them giving me a new start and a second chance. They helped me get my life back on track and become employable.

I went back to school and am now finishing my degree in social work. I became a certified peer specialist, recovery coach, and I'm going to graduate school to get my master's in social work.

I was so fortunate to get hired at Open Arms Housing because I got a job where I like working with people who come from a background similar to my own. I advocate for these ladies. I get them to write their testimonies, their stories. I take them down to the D.C. City Council and I go before the council members and I advocate for them because in a sense, I still believe I'm advocating for myself as well, and I have to be the voice that sometimes they don't have.

But you know, it can be bittersweet at times because I know that contingent upon the type of trauma the individuals have, sometimes they just can't bounce back. That could've been me because it took some time for me to get back on track and I'm just grateful that I didn't become tormented and stuck in all that abuse that I experienced.

How do you deal with a woman who can't bounce back as you say? How do you help her?

I start off basically just asking them simple questions, how they feel, and if it's a negative feeling like anger or anxiety, I pretty much just ask them open and closed questions, like what could we do to help you overcome or what steps would you like to take to change that? I kind of put the pencil and pen in their hand because I don't want to impose or enforce my beliefs on them. I need them to give me what they think will work for them and then I take pieces of it and try to translate it into a way that they will benefit from it.

We had a woman who suffered with a lot of trauma. She was from Ethiopia. I could tell from bits and pieces of her story that she would share with me that she suffered a lot of trauma, abuse and torture. And it took us a while as an agency to even get her connected to an outreach team, an ACT team because she had a lot of issues. There were a lot of services that she could qualify for but because of her trauma, she was paranoid, paranoid about the government. "I don't want them knowing who I am. They're going to do this. They're going to do that." And she would tell me that it wasn't safe and people are going to come and get her. And I realized that was her trauma. That was her traumatic experience that she had over in her country that still was there.

So we worked with her and a case manager on the outreach team came in and really connected with her. We were able to get her a place to live and the services she needed like food stamps and Social Security disability. We were finally able to cross the bridge to get her connected to services. And right now, today, does she still have those traumatic experiences? Yes, she does. But I tell her that I'll protect her. That's the satisfaction that I get out of doing what I do.

But you got to have thick skin being in this work that we do. And it takes a lot of compassion and empathy to work with the ladies who come from a place of homelessness along with trauma.

Everyone needs a home. Everyone needs a roof over their head. Everyone deserves to have a place that they can call home, that they have a key to the door where they can go in and out as they please. I get that. However, my thing with the housing first motto is how do we enhance the quality of their lives? Just giving them housing is not enough because a lot of the ladies, as well as the men, just don't have many life skills. If we just house them and don't make certain things mandatory and don't teach them certain skills, then we're doing a disservice to the population we're trying to reach. You know what I mean?

I do.

I believe that yes, they deserve housing. Let's get them all housed. Let's figure out a way to work with contractors or developers to develop some buildings or just find a big piece of property where you could put so many apartments or apartment buildings on the same property and have the mental health department there where they can go get the therapy they need and have a pharmacist and a medical unit, have all that on one property. Prime example, St. Elizabeth, 801 Martin Luther King, over here in the area where I live. They let their property go to waste because they said they didn't have federal dollars to back it. You could've put everything right there for the homeless. You could've done that. But the people who are making the rules don't understand. They don't understand.

Some of them become hoarders. It's hard to go in and try to help them not hoard because that's like a safety issue, a health hazard and a fire hazard. So yeah, it's always a challenge. We had a woman who was a hoarder. I mean she had so much stuff in her apartment, we couldn't even enter.

Because that's what she was used to doing?

That's what she was used to doing. We would take baby steps with her to kind of like help sort through some of the stuff and get rid of a little bit at a time. If we put it out in our back dumpster, she would figure out a way to go back and get it. Her health started declining because she became diabetic and she wasn't capable of taking her insulin correctly. The ACT team would come out and try to help her. She would get angry, that sort of thing. So we actually had to transfer her to a higher level of care.

Give me two or three things that you want people to know about the experience of homelessness that you think maybe the general public does not know and they should know.

The first thing is that people who are experiencing homelessness, it's not their choice a lot of times. I think people need to understand that just because a person is homeless, we can't guess at why they became homeless. We can't guess at that because nobody knows until you really try to connect with these people to get their side of the story of what happened,

The second thing people should know is that becoming homeless is not an easy task to overcome when you don't have support. You have to provide support for the people who are homeless, and when I say support, I'm not just talking about housing them.

I'm talking about helping them with their trauma or the substance abuse or whatever may have happened for them to become homeless. Let's figure out ways to support them, to give them tools that will give them a better quality of life, give them hope so they can overcome some of these hurdles. We want them to trust people because the biggest problem with homelessness and with people who become homeless is trust. They don't trust anybody. They don't trust people, because something happened for them not to trust people.

And the third thing I think that people should know is that housing them is just not enough. There's other things that need to come into place. At some point, we need to give them a better quality of life, to enhance their quality of life. We have to give them some structure and make some things mandatory when they come into these places of living. It sounds harsh and it sounds like we're taking away their rights but technically we're not. And that's my take. Those are the three major important things that people need to know about homelessness.

Do you think that it's possible in this country to ever end homelessness?

That's a good question. To be honest, I really believe that the government could end it if they really wanted to. Here in the District of Columbia, we've built all these fancy buildings. We've raised the rent sky high. Why can't we build properties for the homeless? Why not? Build some properties for the homeless. You don't have to mix them in. Put them all in one apartment building with separate units.

Look at what we got going on in the city now. I understand about the gentrification, the rebuilding the city, the bringing money back to the city, I get all of that. I understand that totally. But our dilemma here is when you look at Capital Hill, when you look down there by the court building or Indiana Avenue, when you look around, you see people in tents. You see people sleeping on the ground. You just see it everywhere you go. How can you build buildings and don't build any for the homeless?

Can we convert existing buildings for housing the homeless?

Absolutely. We could convert existing buildings as well. Absolutely. Housing. I think that's how we could start to end it, along with having people in place who have enough compassion and empathy to work side-by-side with the less fortunate.

If you got a multimillion dollar grant today, what would you do with it?

I would immediately partner with a developer and try to find some buildings, and they wouldn't be just for housing. I would look for medical. I would look for therapy. I would look for a pharmacist. And invest in that and have it implemented in all the quadrants of D.C. That's what I would do.

What's next on the horizon for you?

I don't know, I don't know. Whatever unfolds for me, I'm willing to dive in. My goal is to someday have a facility of my own to run. That's my goal, seriously.

Well you're on your way.

Yeah, that's my goal. Really thinking hard about doing some proposals, writing some grants and figuring out how I could go through the government to get that done.

Are there any questions that I haven't asked that I should've asked or any other topics or issues you want to share with me?

No, I think we covered a lot.

You're doing some great work. Good for you.

Well, thank you. I really appreciate your interest, I really do.

This is a labor of love for me to be able to talk to people like you and share it with others. The work you're doing is amazing and we need to let people know about it.

Why, thank you. And please feel free to reach out to me anytime.

Thank you Tecoy. Take care.

Okay, you do the same.

Bye now.

Bye.

JIM ZIDAR

Jim Zidar has experienced homelessness for a short period of time. He has been a professional stage, film and television actor for the past thirty-seven years. For twenty-five years, he taught Theatre Arts in grades K-12, including at the International Baccalaureate level. He was listed in "Who's Who in American Education" as one of "the top 5% of secondary school educators."

Jim was a medical counselor and co-administrator at the Bache Memorial Free Clinic in Bethesda, Maryland for five years.

He has worked as an investigative reporter, taxi driver, lumberjack, frame and finish carpenter, jackhammer operator, Teamster freight handler, janitor, and sundry other jobs since the age of fourteen.

Hey Jim, where are you?

I'm in Aspen Hill, Maryland. I'm an Aspen hillbilly.

So how has this pandemic year been for you?

Pretty boring. I mean, I haven't worked since March. I was starting to get a few jobs, and I got caught up with my union dues, and then everything stopped.

Were these acting jobs?

Yeah, acting jobs on films.

So, let's start with the early years. Where did you grow up?

Since I was nine years old, I've lived in this area, in Silver Spring, Maryland, and before that, I was an Army brat, so we moved every couple of years. I lived in Alabama and Maine and briefly in New York and we have family in Canada we go to see every year, and Minnesota.

How old were you when you took an interest in acting?

Thirty.

Oh it wasn't until later?

Right.

And how did that come about?

Well, I was going to Montgomery College and I had thought about majoring in pre-med, so I took some of those courses and worked in a clinic, a volunteer free clinic for five years actually, and ended up co-administering it, and then meanwhile, I got interested in journalism. This was shortly after Watergate and everyone wanted to be Woodward and Bernstein. And I did get a job on Capitol Hill with an investigative reporter that lasted about a year. I got pretty disillusioned with the Washington press corps and the way things seemed to be fixed.

How did you get disillusioned?

I participated in breaking a couple of stories that I thought should have gone to print, but never did because I guess they stepped on the wrong toes.

While I was in college, I was editing the school newspaper, so I used to get press tickets to theater productions all over town, to the Kennedy Center and the National and places, so I would go to those and I'd write reviews to keep up my part in it. And so I went back to that as an interest and went to an acting conservatory where I graduated in 1986.

Where was that?

It was here in Georgetown. It was called the Theater School, and now it's called the Nashville Conservatory of Dramatic Arts, and they had some pretty heavy hitters in the theater school. The president of the school was pretty well connected and I got to study with Davey Marlin-Jones. I don't know if you remember him or not? He was a theater critic and movie critic. He was on television for many years. He wore a fedora and had a mustache and wore a cape.

I remember him.

He was also a brilliant director. He directed nearly a thousand stage shows and operas. He did not work in film, although he was a film critic. He was well-known and respected everywhere. He passed away in 2004, as I was directing my last show at the school where I was teaching, and I actually used my time off and the money I earned from the show to go to his funeral service.

How did you like teaching?

I enjoyed it for the most part. I don't want to go into all the weeds of how I got run out of the school basically by a conservative head of the school, spent about three years doing just that, trying to get rid of me. And when people ask me, I'd say there were creative differences, just that I was creative and he was different.

That's a great line.

Yeah. There's another line that just occurred to me. It's from a Simon Gray play, a British playwright, and it's called Quartermaine's Terms. It's from 1981 or so, and it's about a small public school in Britain where they're trying to get rid of this elderly professor who's beloved by the students, and one character wonders, "Why are school politics so vicious?" And the other character says, "Because there is so little at stake."

That's good.

And true in most cases.

Where were you teaching at the time?

The Washington International School. I'm still in contact with many of my students from back then.

They're in their 40's now. I ran the high school theater department while I was there.

How long were you there?

I was at the school for a total of seventeen years. I had been acting professionally since 1983, and when I started teaching, I just kind of lucked into the job. I beat out people with far better credentials than I had because I was already working there as the headmaster's secretary, and so these kids all knew me.

So let's get into the nitty-gritty. Tell me what your career was like, where you were going, and how and when you first experienced homelessness,

There was a series of bad breaks that a lot of them I don't want to describe, because I will offend people who are still alive.

Understood. Just tell me what you feel comfortable telling me.

My mom died in 2006, and I was taking care of my father the last eight years of his life, and spending less time working and more time doing that. One director in Washington really hated me for some reason, and after he treated me the way he did, I mean, even other actors were astonished at the stuff he would say to me, and I couldn't understand why, but I have not worked in any of those theaters where this director works a lot since then. I'm not paranoid, but I began to think that I was somehow being blacklisted, or I was just not in the club.

So I went out of town and thought maybe it's me, maybe I'm losing my abilities. And I went out of town to audition for Of Mice and Men to play Lenny, and I was hired and it was terrific.

Where was this?

In Newport News, Virginia, at a equity company that was running out of Christopher Newport University, and it was terrific. I became a minor celebrity in the town because of the best reviews I've ever gotten from the local press. I knew that I still had the chops.

But my dad really missed me when I was gone. I'd call him, but I could tell that he was really in rough shape. So anyway, he died in 2014, just short of his 96th birthday. And my siblings, they all wanted to sell his house right away, and a lot of work had to go into it. I lived the closest to there, so I was doing a lot of it, and I used to do that stuff when I was eighteen, but not anymore. I really kind of wrecked myself physically, trying to get this stuff all done by a deadline. So I had some physical deterioration, and that was a summer doing that, and then in October, I got cast and started working that winter on a film of King Lear. I think I sent you a clip from it.

Yes, you did. Very impressive.

Yes, and even there, they had to make allowances for my condition. I wasn't able to run up stairs or that kind of stuff, but they were nice enough to do that. But I'd hoped to use footage from that to get further work. I thought things would work out, but just didn't. Meanwhile, I'm applying for other regular jobs and running into ageism and all this kind of stuff. I was told don't put anything on your resume that's more than ten years old. Well, I have thirty years worth of stuff.

So things just started to slide downhill, and I guess in the summer of 2018, I started to try to navigate the labyrinth of the social safety net, to see if there was anything I could do. I had gotten Medicaid some years before, so I knew a little bit about it, and it was an absolute nightmare. It was like being in a Kafka novel, getting all this information, getting contradictory information.

Yeah, I heard that from the guys at the shelter, almost to the man, about dealing with the bureaucracy, dealing with the healthcare system.

Yes. A lot of the people who work there are conscientious, and they want to do the right thing, but there are some who just seem malevolent. There's this caseworker that I just can't talk to. First of all, he would never answer his phone, ever. I mean he called me once on my cell phone while I was driving, so I pulled over right away, and I called him back within ninety seconds. Wouldn't answer the phone.

Where was this?

Health and Human Services. There was nowhere to go, nowhere to complain about it. This guy would tell me on the phone that I needed this and this and this document, and I needed to bring it to him, or send it to him, but it was safer to bring it and I would say, "Is this all that I need to give you? Are you absolutely sure?" "Yes, yes, that's all." I'd bring it to his office, but he would never see me. I'd have to leave it there. Then I'd get a letter from him in my mailbox asking for three or four other documents that he didn't even mention and the deadline is the next day. And this happened more than once. It's just maddening.

66

Now I'm wrestling with Social Security and Medicaid and the phrase I hear is, "Well I don't work for that agency and I don't know what they require." Well you must have thousands of clients who are dealing with these other agencies because you all send us back and forth among them.

Yeah, how hard would it be for them to find out and to know that so they could help their clients.

Right. You would think it would behoove them to learn something about what the other agencies might need, but it's like they're told don't answer any questions about that, you might be liable or something. Just say, "I don't work for them."

Anyway, I was evicted January 16th, the night of January 16th, for Ayn Rand fans.

Pardon my illiteracy, I'm not familiar with that work. I'm not a big Ayn Rand fan.

Neither am I, but know your enemies.

How long were you at the shelter and what was your impression?

I was there for most of the winter. There were a couple of people working there, really you have to admire them. I know they were paid hardly anything. Even social workers, people with degrees that were getting $15 an hour. I've dealt with many social workers on my parents behalf and on mine. I only met two I think, that I thought were very effective. It seems to me, there's two kinds of social workers, those who can get things done, and those who give you brochures.

All this stuff, it sounds good on paper. They had some housing specialists and the way they would help you find housing was to say, "Go on Craigslist." That was it, and it was up to you to go on Craigslist.

If you were in charge, and you had the budget, what improvements would you make, in any shelter, not just that shelter, but any shelter? What needs to happen?

There were a lot of men who should not have been there, that really needed to be in hospitals, or in psychiatric hospitals, or in some other kind of care. There was a guy who would walk around with urine and feces pouring out of his pants every night, just shuffling around. And they're just being warehoused basically. I don't know whether it can be overcome with training or screening, but it's needed. I'm sure it's hard to get people to work there, but some of the people there really had this attitude that you're a criminal when dealing with us, and you were assumed to be lying all the time, assumed to be scheming somehow. There were some cruel people there too.

I mean, when you would ask for say, a bottle of water, and this woman is writing something on a clipboard, and she goes, "We don't have any." And I can see over her shoulder, a six-foot stack of water bottles in cases.

When I had to be hospitalized for four days when I was there, because one very, very cold night, it was like ten degrees of wind chill, and they have a facility called the overflow. I don't know if you knew about that.

Yes, the bus came every night at nine.

That's right, the bus. So I was lucky enough to have a car, which not many people had, but anyway, I would drive to the overflow shelter. I was told just to follow the bus, so I was always last in line to get in. I was lucky to get a cot to sleep on. So I started driving there. If I got there just ahead of the bus, I would have some chance of getting a regular bunk to sleep on. So I would do that, and there'd always be some kind of trouble on the bus where some knuckleheads would start a fight, and they'd have to either hold the bus up, or pull it over, and there was a cop and all this, and they would not unlock the door at the overflow until the bus got there.

So I got used to waiting outside for a few minutes. But that night there was some big problem with the bus and I'm standing outside in ten degree weather with my pillow while two guys in the shelter are watching through a window, laughing at me, and wouldn't let me in until the bus got there. Another guy showed up, who I guess had gotten there on his own, and finally they let us both in. The next day, I just collapsed. I had to go to the emergency room and thought maybe I had double pneumonia or something. It was totally unnecessary, and that kind of behavior, that lack of compassion among some of the people that work there...

That's shameful.

One of the social workers suggested I check out the shelter in D.C. but I heard there was a lot of drug use going on there. I had heard a lot of bad things about it.

By the way, I'm reading your stage play.

Hope you like it. I remember what a great king you were in my last production with you. I think you'd be a wonderful bishop in this one. Thanks for taking the time to do this interview. Stay safe my friend.

You too.

GORDON BROWN, Ph.D.

Gordon is the founder of A Place to Stand, an organization that helps homeless and low-income families. He was a teacher for more than twenty years and worked in the food and beverage industry.

He developed an affinity for accessing untapped human potential during his teaching career in the U.S. and in an orphanage in Panama.

Gordon's five years as Chief Operating Officer of an international clinical research organization leaves him with contacts of hospital directors and other medical professionals in India, Romania, South Africa, Mexico and Panama.

Gordon holds a Ph.D. in Education from George Mason University.

Hey Gordon, great to see you again.

Good to see you too.

Are you still teaching?

Yes, I've mostly been an educator for the past twenty-five years. I've taught all levels, from elementary school through university. I did a lot of adjunct work at George Mason University. My wife and I lived in Panama for four years and I started a graduate school there with a university in Panama.

Let's start with A Place to Stand. You were the founder of this wonderful organization that helps low-income and homeless people. Tell me about it.

A Place to Stand was really a long time in the making. It started germinating about twenty years ago in my brain. At the time, I lived and worked in Canada and they were claiming that there was no homelessness in Canada. That was just a shock to my system. I was much younger, but I knew better, and I got to thinking, what if there really could be no homelessness? Could that be a real possibility? So that planted a seed.

And then when I was a very young teacher in inner city Washington, D.C., I realized that a lot of our students were coming from difficult family situations. There were a lot of group homes in Washington and some of the students lived in those group homes, and then some were occasionally homeless, either couch surfing or just on the sidewalks, on the streets.

That was around 1997. It was really my teaching experience in Washington D.C. that sort of generated the spark that we've got to do something to house kids and get kids basic needs, because so many of our students didn't have them. They were hungry, they were homeless, so we got involved in the charter school movement, and my wife and I were on an executive charter school planning team that was designed very much like the Seed Academy and others that would be holistic and would be like a boarding school, a residential for public school children.

How would you describe a residential school?

Just like a private boarding school. We came close to enacting this in the state of Virginia, and it would have been the first public boarding school in the state.

So if you think about private boarding schools, like Choate, Andover, Exeter, they could be models for a public residential school like Seed Academy in Washington D.C. They exist, there are just very few of them. You can count them on basically two hands in the country.

The difference is, in my opinion, there should be accommodations for a guardian or parent as needed. So in other words, to house a child and leave a mother on the street is ridiculous, right? Of course. So that would be one minor difference, but it's an easy difference to solve. In fact, it's solving other problems. If every district in this country had one public residential high school, that would go a long way. That's one of many very simple solutions to homelessness.

Then we moved to Panama and we did a lot of this kind of work there. I wrote some grants for a local home for abandoned and abused kids, worked in it for a couple of years, and then saw a version for older children as well. So I got to know programs like that in another country and what they were doing and how Panama dealt with homelessness. My wife was doing similar things with the indigenous population.

And then you moved back to Virginia?

Yes, we moved back to Fairfax County. We were right in the city of Fairfax, one of the wealthiest districts in the nation. What people don't realize about places like Fairfax is that when you have a very wealthy population, you have a service sector. The service sector is often housed in garden apartments, trailer parks that you don't see, or in some cases, unbeknownst to some of the employers, they're homeless.

Once we saw that there was a significant number of families struggling in the wealthiest district in the country, then we decided to get something started. It was when we moved back to Fairfax from Panama that we decided to start A Place to Stand.

What was the reception that you got from local city and county officials regarding funding or zoning or any kind of help that you were trying to get from them?

Before we started, we went up and down the east coast interviewing directors of programs, benchmarking best practices. I volunteered at the men's homeless shelter where you and I met. I went to meetings. We went to Asheville, North Carolina where they virtually eradicated homelessness. We visited a number of those programs and got to know them quite well.

In terms of reception locally, here's the thing. After interviewing directors and meeting and talking with people who have been doing this for five, ten or twenty-five years, we first decided we were going to try to raise money, and initially, the thought was if we could work out a hybrid of public and private funding, that would be optimal. We decided against going the public route for a variety of reasons, and we thought we were going to be able to raise enough money with the board that we put together privately. It turned out we fell short.

Having said that, we recently did get our largest public grant. Part of that is COVID, part of that is that we were so small and flexible that we sort of adapted to doing what we could do. We were also very interested in getting out of our own silo and working with other non- profits and partnering where we could. So I would say we've pretty successfully done that. Often, it takes many years to become established and get the large million dollar plus grants.

Local government basically looked at us and said, look, we all want to end homelessness, but then whenever any of these ideas goes to public hearing, they get shut down. The reception is always pleasant, but let me back up, because I really want to make the point that there are many, many very simple solutions to homelessness. Not only don't they cost anything, they save money. So both the Bush administration and the Obama administration figured this out. They said, when you end homelessness, you save lots of money.

You wrote that the cost to sustain a person in homelessness can range up to $150,000 a year.

Or you can end their homelessness for $13,000 to $25,000 a year. I read more about homelessness than I did for my dissertation. That's based on reports and data that was based on three variables, which were emergency room visits, jail time and emergency shelters.

The econometrics are getting better, more variables are being included, but we're still not really including all the variables. Sometimes housing prices get included, but you need to figure out how to work in things like the stress on the police force, for example, for dealing with homelessness, and the stress on emergency rooms for dealing with homeless people because that's their only healthcare options, so on and so on, plus the diseases of despair that are caused in our society when we don't take care of our own.

In your experience, how do people become homeless?

What surprised me at the men's shelter where I volunteered was that at least half of them are working. It's just that they weren't getting paid enough because we don't have a good minimum wage and we don't have the kind of supports that most developed countries have. They weren't able to pay rent. So, yeah, that was one thing that surprised me.

I've met others who became homeless for the typical reasons, which isn't bad choices, but because of our really horrible healthcare system. One bad accident or illness in the family, often combined with another. Usually, it's a healthcare problem they can't pay for, and then that person who may have been an income earner, whatever it is, broken leg, illness, they lose their job. Now they don't have income, and then something else bad happens, like, whatever, a car transmission or furnace or something goes wrong, and all of a sudden, they can't pay the bills. Next thing they know, they're evicted. It's like a double whammy. There's a family in the school I'm teaching in that just had that happen, and we're trying to help them.

We talked about men's emergency shelters. When you go to a family shelter, it's almost all single moms. The reasons for the homelessness are often illness or an abusive male.

I could tell you inspirational stories for hours, especially about some of my students who got involved in our food program at Malvern High School. I do remember one young woman who came from a middle to upper middle class family. Her father got ill and then he died and they lost an income earner, and it sort of all snowballed. Next thing we know, she and her mother are homeless and they're on the streets.

She was homeless for more than six months. While she was homeless, she got a job at Panera and was showing up to work every day while sleeping in parks on benches. Both she and her mother managed to pull out of it. I got to know them both. There are many stories like that. Unfortunately, there are too many stories like that.

You had mentioned holistic programs. Could you explain what you mean by that?

The problem is, if a person is struggling, and they need to take a bus to go to a program, they can't afford childcare when they have two or three children at home, or three or four children, especially if one of those children has special needs and can't really be left alone. These things are barriers to accessing a program that's two-and-a-half miles away. They're extreme barriers.

So when I say a holistic program, I don't mean that we would provide all of the job training and all of the education programs. What it would mean is that we would do all that we could to provide for them, to make sure that they had the childcare and the transportation covered so that they could get to the program at D.C. Central Kitchen or wherever. They would have what was necessary to overcome whatever obstacles were stopping them from accessing the programs that are already there. Most cities in this country have job training programs, GED programs, English language programs, but getting to them is a problem.

There are people who aren't aware that there are children and families in America who are hungry. In my opinion, those people are ostriches. They're sticking their heads in the sand. *The Washington Post* and other media outlets have done a good job of keeping it in the news. We keep seeing the stat, one in five children are hungry, and there's lots of homelessness. There are constantly articles people like me are writing up. It's in the news. There are documentaries, all kinds of movies. But then, people say, "Oh, but I didn't realize that there were people in my town that were homeless and hungry." Right.

Many of us who enter this field sometimes get cynical, really depressed at the lack of humanity, forethought, intelligence, you know? I mean, again, it saves money to save lives. It's costing us money to let people die in the street, so it can make you cynical pretty quickly. Yet we try to maintain a positive outlook, and become positive forces in this field.

So when I think of all the people who should be giving more, especially people I know personally, yes, that's extraordinarily disappointing. But if you wallow in that, you're not going to last in this field. I think we are very grateful for all the people who have given money and time and resources. This year, because of COVID, people really came out. Lots of people in the community.

Are you encouraged or discouraged with the direction that the country is taking right now in terms of dealing with homelessness? Is it too early to tell with the new administration?

Compared to the last four years, of course I'm encouraged. Again, in this country, homelessness would be easy to solve in so many ways. Let's say there are approximately three million homeless people in this country. That number is so small, that is so easy to solve in so many ways. You don't need new technology, you don't need new ideas, you don't need Gordon Brown. I mean, it's just an easy thing to solve, and it would change the quality of life and you'd find the entire country feeling psychologically better about ourselves, less guilty. We just can't leave our fellow citizens behind and dying on the streets.

What do you think about the tiny house movement for low-income and homeless people?

Personally, I believe we should all be living smaller. We should all have a smaller footprint. So I'm definitely not against the tiny home movement. The question is, can the person or the family coming off the streets be satisfied with a tiny home, and would you or would I be?

In the book, *Mountains Beyond Mountains,* Dr. Paul Farmer talks about the preferential option, that people who have suffered trauma or poverty shouldn't get less than, they should get more than, because what they need is more than. Now having said that, we talk about the holistic piece, the sustainable piece.

Gordon, thanks so much for doing this interview and thank you and Richelle for the amazing work you are doing. Let's get together when you're back in town.

Let's do it. Good luck with the book.

[The following excerpts were taken from blogs published by Gordon Brown.]

Analysis by Nobel winning economist Amartya Sen suggests that famines are not caused by food shortages, but rather food distribution problems. We have plenty of food to feed everyone, we just don't. Furthermore, this failure, which is mostly a failure of our socio-economic and political systems, as well as our collective values, results in more disease, crime, homelessness, despair and death. Thus, again, we are grateful for the volunteerism and support for our efforts to address hunger.

The poverty index is set way too low for a variety of reasons, partly so political leaders can say there aren't too many poor people, and partly so we can spend less on benefits. Hence, unfortunately, despite school breakfast and lunch, children were still coming to school hungry, tired, and sick from malnutrition.

If we want our society to be able to withstand these kinds of shocks with less disruption, we need a more equitable tax and income policy - a more equitable system for stability and strength. A system where nobody has three homes until everybody has one, where everyone has basic needs met, including sufficient nutrition, health care, potable water, and safe shelter. We should focus less on Wall Street and more on Main Street.

A few years ago, we were studying solutions to homelessness in Baltimore, and there was an article in *The Atlantic* that described the incongruity of the existence of thousands of vacant homes in proximity to thousands of homeless persons (for full article go to: https://www.theatlantic.com/business/archive/2014/10/can-homeless-people-move-into-baltimores-abandoned-houses/381647/).

As Rachael Kutler, a community organizer put it, "Clearly there's a moral crisis when you see so many people in need of homes and there's such a glut of vacant ones." As documented by the National Vacant Properties Campaign, vacant buildings result in threats to public safety and a decrease in local property values. Homelessness has a similar impact on communities and much more dire consequences for the homeless themselves. Hmmm: lots of empty buildings and lots of homeless people. What to do? The problem seems intractable and overwhelming. Wait, I'm thinking. I've got it! Perhaps one solution would be to give the vacant buildings to the homeless who could then maintain the properties, and if they need assistance from an organization like Habitat for Humanity or APTS, fantastic. Seriously, this is a no-brainer. No new technology, critical thinking nor genius is required. Bureaucrats and/or property owners simply need to take their pens and connect the dots. It's the right thing to do.

Most of us can't imagine what indefinite homelessness and hunger are really like, so it's hard to empathize. We think it's possible for the homeless to just pull themselves up if they really wanted to. From my work with them, I've discovered it's more like drowning - you can't pull yourself up when your arms are tired already from swimming and there's no one around who can lend a hand. You have no board and no leash to hang on to. Every day you are gasping for breath. Many days you swallow sea water and don't think you'll make it to the next. Many of them don't.

LYNN ROSE

Lynn Rose is Community Engagement Specialist at Montgomery County (MD) Coalition for the Homeless. She develops community and corporate partnerships, supporting over $500,000 worth of in-kind donations and 3,000+ hours of ongoing and single event volunteers, establishing new initiatives to benefit and contribute to the mission of ending homelessness for families, veterans and individuals with disabilities in her community and helping them move forward in ways that allow them to thrive.

Lynn earned a B.A. in History from Wheaton College and an MSW in Social Work from Boston University.

Let's start with the big picture. Describe your mission and your work at the Coalition.

The overall mission of MCCH is very simple. It's to end homelessness in Montgomery County, and for thirty years, our organization has been working with a lot of community partners to try and see that goal accomplished. And what's exciting is we have seen the efforts and the fruits of our labor really show a decline in the number of people experiencing homelessness.

We have a lot of strategies in place that help make that possible, kind of a nice long list of things, but the direct ways that MCCH accomplishes that is through our men's shelter and the veterans' Safe Haven shelter. So that's kind of emergency first step from being unsheltered into shelter.

And then we have about five hundred, over five hundred homes of permanent supportive housing, because we know if we really are going to accomplish an end to homelessness, that includes providing a level of support to the most at-risk kind of families and veterans and individuals that need some rent support and a case manager to help so they don't fall back into homelessness.

We actually have two targeted ways that we are working to end homelessness at MCCH. Those would include our affiliate coalition homes, and they basically buy properties so they will remain affordable and not just affordable for folks that are kind of living with a basic income, but folks that are very, very low income, or maybe have social security disability that they're trying to live on. So lots of those units are reserved for permanent supportive housing. We've got about one hundred units. We're hoping to bump that up to two hundred in the next three years. That's a stretch goal for us because in this county, it's very difficult to have both the finances as well as the properties and have that match at the same time.

It's hard to get the financing at the right time for the particular properties that are available for either right of first refusal or agent. To get that match it's a little bit tricky. And so it's a stretch goal for us, but we know a real important part of ending homelessness is to have those properties that we can maintain and make available for the very, very lowest of income of people in our community.

The other kind of targeted approach to ending homelessness is simple: it's advocacy. We've enjoyed a lot of success in Montgomery County because we get some good support. Both our county government as well as federal government provide a lot of the resources, a lot of the financial resources to support our mission. In addition, they help provide some of the collaboration that is necessary to end homelessness.

I think a lot of times people feel that homelessness is too big a problem, we can't solve it, but it is solvable. And there's about ten ways you can solve homelessness in your community.

One of those is a coordinated entry system. Our county has a coordinated entry system. Everyone who experiences homelessness goes on that list with details. So our organization, our nonprofit, other homeless service providers and the county, we get together every two weeks to say, all right, who's on the list and where can they go? So there's people on a regular basis taking a look at who's actually experiencing homelessness to say who can we pull off the list and put into a home? And then obviously it gives you a sense of who really needs it, what their issues are. And so you've got some good data there to really understand the problem.

The other good thing about a coordinated entry list is it's a real-time list. A regular person in the community can't put someone on the list, but we can say to an outreach team or the 311 number, "Hey, there's someone I think is experiencing homelessness. Can you all go check on that person?"

Who makes that decision?

Yup, I'm getting there. We've got two outreach non-profits who are contracted to do the work in our county. You got to have outreach teams in your community if you're going to end homelessness. So they separate the county in half. The bottom half is Bethesda Cares and the top half is EveryMind. They have staff going out, usually in the evenings, but throughout the day to make sure they're finding people that don't have a home.

I've heard of Bethesda Cares, but what is EveryMind?

They are also a mental health organization. Different organizations have a variety of different programs. EveryMind also runs the suicide hotline. And Bethesda Cares, they have a variety of different programs, so their outreach team is one of the programs they have.

What can we do to make homelessness more of an issue in people's minds? What can we do to make local, state, and federal governments more aware and more engaged?

What can we do to make local, state or federal governments more aware? I think it's advocacy. We can regularly make sure we talk to them and visit them and know who they are and invite them to our events so that they are aware. And it's similar with just regular community members too. We need to give them a sense that homelessness is solvable and that it is the right thing to solve, and that there's a cost that when we don't select homelessness to solve, it costs us. It costs us financially, it costs us as a community. It costs our educational, our correction systems, just a long list of things that it costs us as a community by not solving this problem.

I'll give you a couple examples, one in the health industry. So there's a gentleman that we moved into housing about a year ago. Before we moved him into supportive housing, he experienced chronic homelessness for more than a year and had some kind of a disability. Part of his disability was he had diabetes. He was in the ER, maybe, I don't know, ten, twelve or more times a year for several years. And so that ER visit, he's not paying for that. We're all paying for that. And it's not really substantially improving his health. It's just averting that acute crisis.

Our team member goes with him initially. When he's discharged, he realized he had no idea what they've told him in terms of the discharge instructions. He doesn't understand them. He doesn't feel empowered to say, "Can you run that by me again?" So we're like, "Hey, do you mind? Let's work on this with you. Let's work on managing your diabetes because I don't want you to have to go to the hospital. I know you don't want to go back". He's like, "No, I don't want to go back if I don't have to." So he joins our program and he's not been to a hospital since.

I was recently talking to a fire fighter and a police officer. They are extremely challenged by trying to provide and engage with people experiencing homelessness because they have very little to offer in ways of long-term solutions. But they have to come every time someone says, "Hey, there's someone lying here sleeping in a doorway." So there's lots of costs involved and people need to understand that.

The other thing, honestly, that I think is key is to really take a look at our housing crisis that we're having as a nation, because homelessness is a piece of that, and it really impacts a lot of us.

How does the housing crisis affect us?

The housing crisis is not just affecting the bottom level. It's affecting everyone except for the top levels of people that have lots of resources and can put it into a home. By not providing enough affordable housing units for even the middle income families, we're making it difficult for all of us. So we can restate the issue as a housing issue because affordable housing is such a piece of the problem of homelessness. And solutions are difficult and expensive.

When did you first get interested in the issue of homelessness?

For me personally, I think when I was a kid. It was a long, long time ago and we were just beginning to see homelessness pop up in cities mostly. I remember feeling that's just so terrible, to not have a home because every other part of your life is stuck. I remember really feeling it was something that should be addressed a long, long time ago.

In college, I was volunteering at a women's shelter in D.C., St. Peter's Shelter for Women. It's not there anymore, but it was kind of an overnight shelter. I remember doing some advocacy and just as I engaged with people experiencing homelessness, I realized, wow, there are a lot of problems that are not being addressed that if they were addressed, these people would have homes. I noticed people that were trying their best and going to work and not getting anywhere because they didn't have a home. I noticed people had chronic mental illnesses. Now it's called severe persistent mental illness, like their brain is attacking them and they don't have the right supports and so they don't have a home and they can't earn a living for themselves.

It was just this horrible number of people that were valuable and precious, but were overlooked and having the kind of problems they couldn't solve on their own. And then what's even worse, they were getting blamed for it. There's still that underlying thought that if you don't have a home, you probably are a drug addict or an alcoholic, and you probably made a bunch of bad choices. I start by telling people that actually it's more of a problem once you fall into homelessness to develop a substance abuse issue, than before you fall into homelessness, because all of us, when we're stressed, if we enjoy a drink and we're really stressed, we might have two. So imagine if you have no home and no prospects and no nothing, you're absolutely going to turn for comfort in ways that are maybe not healthy for you.

I know some of the guys at the shelter occasionally would go outside and pass a joint and I guess my responsibility as a volunteer was to turn them in, but I just didn't have the heart.

You did exactly the right thing. A low barrier shelter allows you to just say, "I am here for this role to be supportive and engage with people. And I can just tap out after that, in a good way." Yeah, you did the right thing.

You also talked in your lecture about the issue of racial equity and homelessness. Can you summarize that for me?

It's such an important question. And literally, we could talk for the next two hours and I wouldn't even begin to touch it. The number of people experiencing homelessness who are Black is outsized compared to the number of people in our community who are Black. And that is a big part of lots of barriers, historically, from redlining, lack of access to resources, no trickle down. Nobody's family is able to pass on any wealth. You're not given employment at the same rate that other people are. You're not given as great an education. There's all these ways that racism impacts people's opportunities and closes doors.

So there's a huge connection between the impact of racism and the number of people who are Black that experience homelessness. You're looking for a landlord, you're looking for a job and those are still going to be barriers to your opening and walking through that next door. There's so many kinds of things that create this massive problem. We see it in who we're serving. And we have for a number of years.

Your Coalition talks about ending homelessness in the county by 2023. Is that realistic? And if it is, how are you going to go about it?

Well, I have to say ending homelessness by 2023 looked a lot more promising before we had a pandemic, although our annual count isn't significantly higher this year during COVID. People who do research about these things are reporting that there likely will be an increase in the number of people experiencing homelessness as we move forward.

But how do we do it? We do it in the same way that we did for veterans. We started a target, because this is the federal best practice, to start with a subpopulation of people experiencing homelessness. We pulled out our list of people that we knew, because it's a real-time list on our coordinated entry system, and we found every single veteran who was homeless and found homes for them all. That takes a lot of resources, a lot of coordination. And then we rallied our networks, our community support, our different organizations. That's how we did it for veterans. Obviously, it doesn't end all homelessness for veterans but it's a much more manageable level. So that is certainly possible as we move forward with the other subpopulations.

The next sub-population is the chronic homeless – people chronically experiencing homelessness over a year and often with a disability. There are a number of people who fit in that category.

But again, we do it block by block. We've been for the last year focused on families as a community, ending homelessness for families. A lot of coordination, a lot of resources, a lot of focus went into that and we've been able to kind of get it down. One of the interesting things is we have not yet seen a huge increase in families seeking homelessness assistance. In part, I'm sure that is because families are double and tripling up in households right now because the last place you want to be during a pandemic is in a shelter. We've got a lot of families that are losing their housing that are not having great housing choices. They're thinking, "I'm going to now live in a room. I'm going to live in someone's family room or living room and the kids will be in the bedroom and I'll sleep on the couch."

Those people are not counted as people experiencing homelessness because they're in a house, but that's happening more often with families at this point. So we're not seeing a huge increase. Our focus is to help our families stay housed and stay safe during the pandemic. So for the three hundred kids that we support, our focus has really been how do we help you all stay safe and sane. Honestly, during this pandemic with everything shut down, it's been a lot of extra pressure.

How does Montgomery county compare in terms of its efforts to end homelessness with other jurisdictions in the country?

That's a great question. So when we ended, as a county, veteran homelessness, we were one of only four in the entire nation to do it. Talk about being part of a leading county, a leading community ending homelessness!

I'll give you another little anecdote. I think you remember both of these people, Ace and Courtney, at the shelter. Ace was our operations mandate manager for like fourteen years. And then Courtney was there for, oh, I don't know, six or seven years. Both of them, because it was actually closer for them, ended up taking jobs in a Virginia shelter. And both of them reported back that Virginia was about five years behind where MCCH was. So I think we've been able to push forward and keep pushing forward and basically try things that would work and leave the stuff that's not working behind and keep doing the stuff that's working.

I remember how good the food was at the shelter.

Yeah! I mean the fact that we've been around a long time and we let people know our needs and we kind of developed a system. So I'm responsible for, I don't know, thousands of meals a year at the men's shelter. The only reason I can do that and still breathe every day is because we've got volunteer groups that are willing to prepare meals, deliver them and serve them.

So because we run the men's shelter, we were a huge source of distributing funds from federal. Federal goes through the county and works with our teams to get the guys out of the shelter, into a home. In the last six months, we have over one hundred fifty guys moved out of the shelter into homes. A lot of those are rented rooms, because the rented room is the new efficiency.

We were gradually picking up the pace, but man, we've kicked it into overdrive. Part of that was having those connections with the county and being trusted by the feds to be able to distribute the money. In addition to our staff, we had an additional eleven people that were in the field, kind of working at the shelter, getting people to go.

I'll tell you my vision. I would love someday for us to be not an incubator, but kind of like a site where people come visit and they get to think and envision and dream about how do we take some of these strategies back to our community or fill in the gaps. Maybe our community has two of the ten or eight of the ten, but we need to work so that we've got all of the ten and we can be even more successful.

They need to come and learn and be inspired. There needs to be kind of a workshop and then they can be sent back wherever they came from. We're the largest in Montgomery County that's solely focused on homeless services, but we work with a lot of people so we've got to collaborate a lot to get things done.

My background in social work has been very helpful plus my real passion for ending homelessness for everyone because it's the right thing to do and it makes economic sense for our community.

Thank you Lynn. Thank you for all the good work that you do.

Thanks so much Deno.

CLIFTON THOMPSON

Clifton Thompson, known as Givon, is an artist living and working in the Washington, D.C. area who has experienced homelessness.

His artwork uses the aesthetic elements found in African woodcarving to produce stunning three-dimensional effects. The art is intricate and unique with metaphysical undertones and wonderful graphic complexities, including timeless hieroglyphic depictions from some ancient time. And yet it's contemporary, compelling you to study it and try to figure it out. Givon's work is masterful, full of depth and meaning, and has sustained him through periods of homelessness.

Where were you born and raised? Where did you go to school?

I was born in Washington, D.C. I'm a third generation Washingtonian. My parents and grandparents grew up in the Georgetown area and part of Bethesda. I have people that resided in this area, particularly off of the River Road area, as far back as slavery.

My neighborhood was comprised of home owners and everybody respected everybody. It was almost like a rural part of town. We did things the way people in the country did, leaving doors unlocked, things like that.

I was one of six children raised by my mom and dad in a duplex house. Next door was my uncle's family. So I grew up alongside my six cousins.

My parents' motivation was to make sure that we were well-rounded, properly raised, that we had a roof over our heads, never wanted for anything and were well-taken care of. I came from a very loving family.

Tell me about the schools you attended.

I went to the local elementary school and junior high school, but I didn't want to go to the local high school, so I took a test to go to McKinley Tech because I aspired to become an artist, influenced by my parents and my uncle next door.

That was my next question. When did you know that you wanted to be an artist?

I aspired to become an artist as a child, being influenced by my mother, my father, and my uncle next door. I was about maybe four or five at the time. My mom would take these breaks from time to time from washing and cleaning in the middle of the day.

And one day she asked one of my brothers to bring a friend of his across the street over because she wanted to draw a picture of him.

I didn't know she had taken an art correspondence course that my dad had bought for her. And then I saw her with a pencil draw an image of our neighbor, Ronald, while he sat for a few minutes. And when she finished, I was in awe. To me, it was magical that with a pencil, she drew an image that looked like a photograph, and I knew that's what I wanted to do.

I'll never forget that. It was in our back room addition, which was like our rec room. And when she did it, I began picking up pencils and drawing just out of my head, trying to draw things I looked at. I remember even in the first grade, one of our projects was to draw a map from our bedroom to our classroom. And I was able to picture, almost like a bird's eye view, what it was like to go out from my front door, go down the street, turn the corner, make it over to the school, and go through to our classroom. I was learning to develop mental pictures.

That is very important for drawing, having images in your mind. My uncle was a professional photographer, and in his leisure, he would carve wood as a hobby. And I remember being around ten-years-old watching him carve these African masks. And for some reason, it just grabbed me that my uncle did this, and there was something about it that was mysterious. I consider that as the seed planted of me doing the African expression I'm developing right now.

Well it sounds like to me that artistic ability was in your DNA. Did you study art in school?

Oh yes. I took this workshop just north of Howard University. It was called the Workshops for the Careers in the Arts, WCA. It was sponsored by George

Washington University, but a lot of the instructors came from Howard. My sculpture teacher, painting teacher, some of the dance instructors, some of them well-known to this day, they were part of that workshop. They sat us down near the middle of 1974, my senior year, and told us that that workshop was slated to become Duke Ellington School of the Arts. I learned how to paint starting at that workshop. And I did a little bit of sculpture there too, messing with plaster. I was on my way to becoming an artist.

Tell me about the period of your life right after you graduated.

My young adulthood was comprised of a series of things which actually were directed by two major forces in my life. One was the art, and the other was my spirituality. At fifteen, when I was in the ninth grade, I had a brother that died, my older brother. He was five years older than me. That shook my world in the most tragic of ways. He died from a blood disorder that I have now, which is a gene mutation that causes excessive blood clotting.

And so that took him out. And that particular event spurred me to want to know everything about God, humanity, why there's evil, why people do what they do. It was like I had a personal mandate to want to know about life, period.

And this is pre-internet, so everything depended on what I grabbed, what I read, who I worshiped with, all of that, which affected my whole direction in life. Everything was about seeing life through the lens of the belief that there's a spiritual world and how people are governed by that in their day-to-day human existence.

Art was what I knew I always wanted to do, and it was a way to express my inner world as well. So everything that I did after my senior year was shaped by that.

Did you start working right after school?

Yes, I basically took on different jobs. I did things because I wanted to rub elbows with life, and I wanted to be able to create and express life.

And of course, you continued painting.

I wound up painting with one of my father's friends who had these painting contracts all over the D.C. area. I did portraits for a time until I realized I couldn't make a living off of it. I told myself I always wanted to be an artist, but if I couldn't, I would become a trucker, because that would afford me greater exposure to the world.

Many years later, I became that trucker and traveled the forty-eight states and got exposed to so many things.

At what point in your life did you experience homelessness for the first time?

The very first time was actually up in Baltimore. It was in 2011. I was working as a trucker for FedEx making good money, but my mother was ill and I couldn't do the job and take care of her. I wasn't getting enough rest. With a trucker, you have to have your rest, and I was coming in 6:30 in the morning pulling a load from Harrisburg, Pennsylvania, and drowsy. And I could have easily had my license taken away because DOT spot-checks truckers all the time. So I quit my job to take care of my mother, taking her to her doctor's appointments, feeding her, bathing her and everything. And she needed some surgeries, knee surgeries and eye surgeries. Then my sister retired and she and my mother both moved to Florida. I left that household and was living in my car.

I tried to get back into trucking, but the trucking industry was so impacted by the 2008 recession, they had changed a lot of the rules. I had sleep apnea at the time and had a sleep machine. I couldn't get back into trucking where I could have made money to support myself.

A friend of mine owned a bunch of properties up in Baltimore and so he had a place for me to stay while I worked on his properties. I sanded floors, painted houses, emptied trash, did any odd-end jobs for him in exchange for having a place to stay, which was what I wanted so I could focus on my art. But I was working so hard at times, I didn't have time to work on my art because I needed to sleep for the next day.

In 2011, I got ill. For some reason, I don't know what happened to my body, but I was worn out and I told my friend, I said, "Hey man, I can't work for you anymore because it takes two or three days just to recover from anything that I do for you." If I'm moving cinder blocks or something, I was aching not only the next day, but the day after that and the day after that. I didn't know what was happening to me. The doctors couldn't tell me what it was. All I knew was that I couldn't exert much strenuous force or energy. My friend told me I could stay in one of his properties up North Baltimore and just make sure it wouldn't be broken into or catch on fire.

So I stayed in that house and just drew, drew, drew, developed my stuff. I made so much headway because I couldn't do anything else. Technically I was homeless, but I had a place to stay. I had food stamps. I had enough money to take care of my food needs, but that was controlled homelessness.

At the end of 2011, I came to D.C. because both my parents had passed away in December. So after the funeral service, instead of going back to Baltimore, I went to visit my daughter in Virginia. She was in high school at the time, and I was able to stay with them. I was going to stay with them for a week and then go back to Baltimore, but I became such a part of their household, my daughter's mother begged me to stay. My daughter was a swimmer and her mother was the swim coach.

And so I stayed with them for a couple of years. But then for some reason, my daughter's mother lost her house. They had to go into a shelter situation and I was left homeless. I was able to sleep in her van that she wasn't using. During the day I would go to the library and study. And I had a friend that let me use their bathroom to take a bath, shave and everything, do laundry. But I was living out of a rolling luggage case.

Then I got sick again with my embolism. It was late 2013. I had to go to the hospital for them to monitor my blood condition.

Is there a name for this condition?

It was called a type three gene mutation, and it starts from a deep vein thrombosis, a blood clot traveling from the leg up to the lungs. My body overproduces clotting. And those clots ravage the system where it's clogging up the lungs. You could get strokes from it. You can get a heart attack from it. The closest thing I had was a lung embolism where it cut off my air. And because it came from the left leg, it was less likely for me to have a stroke. If it came from my right leg, it was very likely I would have had a heart attack and a stroke because of how the arteries run through the body from those legs. So after that hospital stay, I stayed with my other sister in Hyattsville, until she got prepared to go to Florida to live with my other sister.

I didn't have a place to stay because I didn't have a job. I was officially homeless. I actually went down to the Huntington Metro and asked one of the bus drivers, "Where's the nearest shelter?" And he knew, he said, "Man, I'll take you there. I'm going straight down route one, towards Fort Belvoir. There's a shelter, people go in there all the time."

Tell me about your experience at the shelter.

The day I went into the shelter, they just so happened to be taking what they call overflow. The shelters have a certain quota of people and they turn people away once they get their quota. But the day I came was the day they had some extra beds available. And two days later, I got a permanent bed. One of the guys there told me, he said, "Man, you're one lucky guy. It doesn't happen like that. Sometimes it takes months to get a bed. But you got one in two days." I said, "Well, I'm going to tell you, man, whoever's upstairs is always looking out for me."

How long were you there?

A few months. I got a job through the shelter. You go to this place where you get online and you can do your job search during the day. I wound up getting a job working for a taxi company. Once you get a job from the shelter, they have a housing locator arm where they find rooms and everything for you. The people at the shelter found a room for me. I was back on my feet thanks to that shelter. They were set up to do that. And they had a class called Up from Poverty. They had two teachers that raised questions for us as to what we wanted to do, where do we want to go, how do we get there and they let us know what we needed to do. But not everybody in the shelter took those classes. Some had mental issues. They were pretty much permanent wards of the state. Some were just elderly, sick or disabled. There were four classes of people there -- people like me who just fell through the cracks, people who had mental instability issues, people who had physical disability issues, and then there was the prison population. Some of them couldn't find jobs, so they were down on their luck.

I saw these four sets of people in the shelter system, but those who were like me, they wanted the jobs and to get out of there. You knew who was in what category while you were there.

There were some guys in the prison situation, you'd never know they came from prison unless they told you because they were cultured, determined and focused on getting on their feet, and the shelter helped them to do so. Some of them got really good jobs.

Now my second stint, bona fide stint of homelessness, happened after I had my cab job. I became really good friends, the best friend I ever had, with one of my cab fares. We had so much stuff in common. It was like we just had this kindred spirit, like I had known him all my life.

He knew seven languages. Everywhere he went, he could talk to people in their language. Not this, "Hi, how you doing," but serious conversation. He spoke to people in Arabic. He spoke to people in Spanish and French, Russian or whatever. I was in awe of that and he was in awe of me doing art. I felt like we were going to see the world together. It was just that strong a bond.

He had a disabled wife who he was taking care of, but then he got sick, wound up in the hospital and asked me to take care of his wife. So I started taking care of his wife until he got better, but he didn't. Three weeks later, he died. For the next three years, I took care of his wife until she had gotten so sick she had to go to the hospital. The wife, or now the widow, went to a nursing facility for rehab for a whole year. I had to go back to the shelter.

And I think that's when we met, at the shelter.

Right.

And you told me you were taking tests to get back into trucking.

Yeah. I had to take an online questionnaire to see if I was eligible, because with my age, I was in my sixties, so they were concerned if I could get behind a wheel of a truck. I told them, I still knew how to drive. I wasn't disabled or anything.

You told me that when you were at the Virginia shelter, they had asked you to speak on their behalf. What was that all about?

There were like four or five shelters in the Northern Virginia area. They'd had this dinner at some place, I forgot where, that some of the people representing each shelter would come. Every shelter had to have one representative stand up and tell where they came from, how they got into the shelter system, how it worked for them and how they got out. I was asked to speak for our shelter.

People were saying how they came from abusive households, how they came from the foster system, were on drugs, wound up in a shelter. But I didn't come from all of that. When I got up, as I was walking toward the podium, I thought to myself, I'm gonna paint another picture of homelessness, and I told them my story.

What did you tell them?

I told them I came from a good family. I was educated, everything was happening well for me. I had a daughter who I loved. I had all these good things happening, but then I fell through the cracks.

I was telling them how there's a lot of people in the shelter who just simply fall through the cracks. They had well-paying jobs, some of them even degrees, but they just fall through the cracks.

I told them how that Virginia shelter helped me and other people get back on our feet because we needed the help. We didn't have anywhere to go. I thanked the shelter organization for what they did and I thanked some of the residents, because we were actually helping each other too.

Did the shelter help you get back into trucking?

The Rockville shelter did. They were able to fund me for whatever I needed to get back into trucking and also accept and factor into it the expectation of possible failure. Some people lose jobs for whatever reason. For some, the job didn't work out. Sometimes someone has a falling out with the managers and it takes a while to get another job, but the rent is still due.

Let's wrap this up with a big question: What can we do as a society, as individuals, as charitable organizations, as local, state and federal governments, what can we do to ultimately end homelessness in this country? What are some things that need to happen based on your knowledge and experience?

One is to really identify those four groups I was talking about. And among those four groups, see who are the people who are capable of standing on their feet if they get the proper help. The ones who can't stand on their feet, you got to find a way to make sure that they are not a problem for the rest of the community. Those who are mental, get the mental treatment. There's a lot of mental cases that need more treatment than just housing.

For those of us that fall through the cracks, there needs to be some type of financial assistance to help us get back on our feet and then follow up on those people to make sure they're doing what they're supposed to do. Because once you do a tally of that and see the record of successes and everything, then they'll know what's working and what's not.

I think the problem with the shelter system is they're very reluctant to give out money because they're afraid people may use it to do drugs or be frivolous with it and not use it for what they're supposed to. But if the shelter people have a follow-up where they make sure these people do what they say, then I think they'll be more apt to actually give people what they need. For example, there was an event at Howard University that, if I had been able to print up my work and been a vendor down here, I could have made several thousand dollars in a weekend. But they weren't willing to fund my art supplies and so I missed that event. The important thing is to recognize where there is a need and try to help in some way.

There needs to be a realistic look at what goes on in a human being's life for them to get back to normalcy. And from my point of view, Congress and governments have been penny pinching when it comes to basic needs.

I don't know how people can do it, but they need to recognize that life goes by so fast, and that blinds us from the needs of other people. We may wish to help people, but we just don't have time. I don't know how that can be remedied, but that's what's needed. People need to slow down so that they can take time and look around because we are in a society where we have access to a lot of information, which is why this book and all this is important. People are reading, people are gathering information, learning, and they need to know. And that's the challenge. But I'm hopeful. I think we can end homelessness in our lifetime.

Givon, thank you so much for taking the time to talk with me. Your life story is compelling and your ideas thoughtful, compassionate and practical. I can't wait to share them with others.

Thanks Deno.

ASHLEY McSWAIN

Ashley McSwain is Executive Director for Community Family Life Services in Washington, D.C. Prior to joining CFLS, Ashley served as Executive Director for Our Place D.C., a nonprofit providing programming and resources to currently and formerly incarcerated women in the D.C. area.

Ashley is a licensed Social Worker in the state of Maryland and in the District of Columbia. She holds a Master's of Social Work from Temple University, a Master's of Organizational Development from American University, and a Bachelor's degree in Criminal Justice from Temple University.

She is a member of the adjunct faculty at Catholic University in the Graduate School of Social Work and is certified as a domestic violence counselor. She has worked in the human services field for more than twenty-five years.

When and how did you get involved in social work?

I used to be a probation officer early in my career. And a lot of what you see is people who are homeless and the probation services are not really designed to deal with social needs of clients. So I left probation and went to a nonprofit that was serving homeless families.

How did you start out?

I started out as a case manager and moved my way up to a director. And I realized that there were just a lot of barriers to people who were homeless, and I felt like it was something that I was skilled enough to help with. That's how I got involved with homelessness. I did that for ten years, in Bucks County, Pennsylvania. I grew from being a program manager to overseeing all of the shelters and all of their transitional housing programs, all of their food pantries, all of their first-time home buyer programs and their EMAP [Emergency Management Programs] program.

When you first encountered homeless individuals, what were some of your initial reactions?

Well, one of the things I originally believed was that homelessness was a devastating issue and that everybody who was homeless was navigating to get out of it. And I thought that was their primary goal, that was their primary objective -- to figure ways to get out of it. What I've learned was that there were some families who had generational homelessness and this was a lifestyle. For example, I remember talking to one of my clients and she said, "We'll look for a place in the summer and in the winter we can do transitional housing," and right then in that moment, I realized that it's not that she wants to be homeless. It's just that this was a lifestyle right now. And that was new information to me.

And then I remember talking to another woman who was homeless and she had worked all of her life and had a pension. I remember telling her we're going to call and we're going to get this pension, get access to this pension right now, because she needs it now. And I remember her saying, "Girl, after this shelter, I'm going to go to the Red Cross, and then I'm going to my daughter's. I'm tired." It wasn't that she didn't have the desire to get to some housing, she just was tired. And the urgency that I felt was different from hers. I realized that I can't want something more than my clients and that I have to be where they are and not where I want them to be.

Was there anything in your education that helped prepare you for these encounters and these attitudes?

No, not really. I'll be honest with you. One of my degrees is in organization development and that particular degree was what really helped me fully understand the experience of homelessness. Being able to really look at this experience from someone else's lens, as opposed to my own. Your social work degree is designed to help you respond to crisis and to remove barriers, but they don't do a very solid job of helping you understand a person's lived experience. And that is what you are doing with case management, dealing with not just their homelessness, but their lived experiences, their feelings around their experiences, their feelings about being homeless.

You would think that your degree in social work would address those things, but not so much, not so much. The other thing I learned, and I don't know if I learned this from school, is that I remember working with the accountant and she never seemed to understand why I wanted to spend money on things. And in that moment, I realized you don't understand homeless people. That was when I decided that the entire organization needed to be educated on the experience of homelessness, so when I asked for money, there would be some understanding of what the money was for and why I needed it, so I wouldn't get the pushback I was getting.

That was when I pursued the organizational development degree. I started training the organization about homelessness and it was transformational. The people in the organization, the accountant, the bookkeeper, everybody that wasn't doing direct services needed to understand homelessness. And once they did, then my work as a social worker became easier. So when I asked her for money, she knew why. It made sense why. The organization needs to be on board with supporting the needs of their constituents, not just the case managers. Does that make sense?

It makes a lot of sense. There are so many misconceptions about homelessness.

Right, so many misconceptions out there. One of the misconceptions that I learned was that homelessness was a result of some mistake a person had made or some personal choice that they had made. But then, when I started doing this work, I encountered things like generational homelessness as I mentioned. I would see women coming into the program with their children and then I would see their children come in with their children who were homeless. I was there long enough to see that.

And generational homelessness isn't anybody's fault. If my mother was homeless then chances are that I'm going to be homeless too. And so it's not a personal flaw. I don't know that I was clear about that when I first started working with this population.

I understand. I had a lot of misconceptions when I started out as a volunteer. What have been some of the more satisfying stories and clients that you've worked with? I'm sure there are many.

Yeah, there are many. I started doing this work in '97, '98 with homeless people, and I still have some of my clients who are reaching out to me even today. They found me on Facebook and many of them are gainfully employed. I had a client reach out and she talked about how meaningful her time with me was. And she was in a really good place. She was stable and getting married. And man, that just makes me feel like I made a difference.

I've had clients go from being homeless for years to now having husbands and houses. I remember one time I had this client in the shelter. She had four kids and she just would not do any of the things that I suggested. So I talked to her and I worked with her and then we had to ask her to leave because her time was up. She wasn't making progress. She wouldn't follow through. And I'm telling you, it couldn't have been more than a month later, she called me up and said, "I was just calling to let you know that I'm in school now. And I got housing and I did all the things that you and I talked about."

And then I had another client with five or six children. I'll never forget her. She was addicted to crack off and on. She was in the shelter and then we got her into housing but then she relapsed and was homeless again. And when she came back into the shelter, man, she was working hard. I remember her. She was walking I think a mile to work. And then she had a daughter who was graduating and going to college and I remember using all of my resources to help her daughter get to college. I bought her computers and all the things she needed to set her dorm up. And I remember when I was leaving the organization, how I set them up to continue to support her, because I was doing stuff that the program didn't really do, but I knew she needed that kind of support. I was so proud of that family, to see her daughter go to college and to see her get clean and sober again. And so that really warms my heart when I remember those experiences.

There's just been so many moments of celebration and sometimes it's not just because they got housing, but they completed a degree or a program they were trying to do or they got a GED. I had one client who was challenging, but the system that she was working in seemed angry at her. And I remember them saying that she's not going to get her GED, couldn't do it. I remember tutoring her and she got her GED. Must've been in thirty days. The people who were supposed to serve her, who were so negative, had to eat those words when she got that GED in thirty days.

There have been a lot of moments where clients come back and want you to know how well they've done, or they come back and share with you how something you said made all the difference to them. I had a client, a student, reach out to me maybe six months ago and all she said was, "I'm working in this organization and I've thought about you and I wanted to reach out and let you know how much of a difference you've made in my life." I've got lots of stories like that.

I bet you do. Why don't you write a book?

Well, I did start writing a book. I have my own personal journey. Maybe I'll talk to you about it one day.

Absolutely. I would love that. Can you talk about the differences in how homelessness affects women versus men?

Very differently from the way it affects men. And I remember when I was a probation officer, I would have women who never seemed to be compliant. They always had some drama. And I did not understand why women who are on probation are harder to work with than men. That's all I knew. I didn't have any context for why. I didn't have any rationale to explain what the phenomenon was. I just knew that women were harder to work with than men.

And so, one of the things I've come to learn and know is that women have quite a few different barriers than men have. And if you're going to work with this population, you have to acknowledge those barriers. One issue was children. Women are the primary caregivers of their children. So being homeless is harder to resolve when you have children and all of the issues that come with having children. And then I also realized that women have trauma. Many of the women that I've worked with have experienced trauma during their childhood or as adults -- domestic violence, sexual violence, childhood adversity. Those things have to be acknowledged if you're going to work with women who were homeless.

And then this idea that women are relational. When you are in relationship with women, they'll listen to what you have to say. But if you're just given directives and you haven't established any kind of relationship, it's hit or miss. They're never going to listen to you. Those are the things that came into view at some point. And once they came into view, I was able to really approach them in a way that was more successful. It matters that you are in relationship with women. It matters that you acknowledge that they have children and it matters that you understand their trauma.

Are all your clients women?

That's our target audience. We have one program where we work with men, but for the most part, our target is women.

How does the experience of homelessness affect the children?

It is, for those clients who themselves don't have a good foundation, very difficult for the children. One of the most difficult situations I've seen was a client who was just belligerent and difficult and seemingly only cared about her own experience. She was in the shelter, in the program. She had been there for years and it was time for her to leave. I mean, we're talking four years. It was time for her to go, but she refused to do anything. I said, "We're going to have to evict you because you have to go." Her response was, "I'm not going anywhere." She was just angry and she was not going to do anything to help her own situation. She's like, "Fuck you, I'm not going nowhere." I'm thinking, wow, you got to go. This is a temporary program. You were only supposed to be here two years. She was there four years. And she would not do anything to make her son's life manageable.

I remember when the sheriff came to take her things. Her son was sitting on the sidewalk watching them. He was devastated. And I remember us telling him that he could reach out directly to us if he ever needed anything. It was heartbreaking because she had a son who was getting ready to go to high school and she refused to take any proactive action.

I remember us all wanting to cry because he was a really good kid. And he had to sit by and watch the sheriffs come in and remove his items. It could have been avoided had mom behaved differently. So mom's behavior is what dictates the grounding of the children. I have seen families where mom had a sense of self. Mom was not defined by her homelessness and the children were supports for mom. The children were looking out for mom. Children seem to understand their circumstances and can help mom.

Clients who don't have any sense of self, who don't have any kind of grounding can't prepare their children to navigate the experience they are having. And so the kids seem aimless. They seem to be unaware of why they have to keep moving. So when mom is grounded and able to communicate with her children, the children seem to fare better. When mom doesn't acknowledge the reality of her experience, the children do poorly.

What's the status of local and federal programs for the homeless?

They have lots of different programs -- transitional housing, rapid rehousing, but all of those things are temporary and there aren't enough of them. You can't interrupt generational poverty and generational homelessness with temporary housing. There are some families that have limitations that will never be resolved. Minimum wage jobs are not going to pay the rent. People need subsidies, and not because they don't want to work, but because minimum wage doesn't afford them a living wage to pay for housing.

So homeless people get blamed for their inability to get out of homelessness, even when the job that they have to take doesn't afford them enough money to pay for housing. It is a vicious cycle, and it's unfair to judge people when the system is designed to keep them in this cycle. How am I supposed to get out of homelessness if the jobs that are available to me don't pay me enough to pay for housing? So that's the system right now that we're in. In D.C., housing is $1,200. Minimum wage in D.C. is fifteen dollars an hour, but that's still not enough to make a $1,200 payment if you got transportation and food and childcare and all of those things.

Why isn't homelessness an issue for most politicians?

Because politicians don't want to allocate money for homelessness when they and the voters believe homelessness is the fault of the homeless. People need to understand that there are systemic reasons why people are homeless. When you blame the people who are suffering, then nothing ever changes. You have politicians who think people are homeless because they made bad choices. They were drug addicts or whatever. And as long as people feel that way, then there is no benefit to advocating for housing. So if there was a way to shift that understanding, then politicians will have some cover because they always need cover in order to advocate. We at CFLS [Community Family Life Services] have the speakers bureau and that was all about having people with lived experience tell their stories to help change the thinking among people who don't understand. It's not enough to lobby for housing. You have to change the narrative and take it away from blaming people for their circumstances and acknowledge that some of these circumstances are systemic, generational. I think that if that can happen, then change can happen.

Can you give me examples of those systemic circumstances?

The GI Bill that African-Americans and minorities were excluded from. The redlining where people were segregated and treated like sub-humans. Jim Crow laws. All of those things have an impact on people building wealth.

When the war was ending, there was this opportunity to help people build wealth and get access to housing, but minorities were excluded from it intentionally. They were relegated to other communities, or you had a government that would build these projects but then wouldn't maintain them. You got people living in a great project, new apartment, new housing, but then the government wouldn't maintain it, so that it declined and then the tenant was blamed. It's a lot of those stories that perpetuate this idea that poor Black people are the problem.

I read that it costs $65,000 or more a year in taxpayer dollars to support a homeless person. But it costs around $15,000 to provide housing for that person. Is that correct?

Yes it is. It is. And just look at all of the abandoned homes. The thing that kills me is that you have all these landlords who take poor care of their properties and then blame the tenants. You have residents in the District, in Philadelphia, in Walter Moore and multiple communities where people are living in rented housing and the landlords aren't caring for the units. It's predominantly Black communities where repairs aren't being done.

With all these abandoned houses around, there's housing stock that's available. There's tons of housing. But it's the will and the funding. I used to do elder care and I used to do home business in the community. I would go into blocks sometimes where fifty percent of the houses were abandoned. Why shouldn't those houses be transferred to livable units? I mean, you can walk around D.C. and see available abandoned housing. Why can't we just rehab those houses and put homeless people in them and help them? Maybe the rent should be income-based. Why wouldn't we do that? These houses are vacant, but there isn't a will right now for that. You have to lobby for changes in the thinking.

Then you look at the tax base. In poor communities, things don't happen. There are a lot of systems that keep minorities who are homeless oppressed, or keep them homeless. And that's not the same as advocating anybody's individual responsibilities, because I run into a lot of sisters that are trying to manage their responsibilities, but this system is bigger than them.

Tell me more about your speakers bureau. How many people do you have doing that and how is it working for you?

Right now we've trained about sixty women to speak about their lived experiences. And so all over the DMV [D.C., Maryland and Virginia area], we have organizations that hire them to tell their story. We train them to learn how to tell their story. There is a model that you use to tell your story. We pay women twenty-five dollars an hour to go through a training to tell their story. And then after that training, they get paid by various venues as an expert to tell their story.

So we've got conferences that hire them and organizations and universities. They're hiring them to tell their stories.

When did you start it?

I started it when I was the executive director of a nonprofit. Women were coming out of prison and I remember them telling me that they were asked to speak publicly. And I remember they were doing it because they were hoping it would lead to maybe money or maybe it would lead to a job. But it never did. And I said that I would, if I ever had the opportunity, pay women to tell their stories. And so in 2018, I went to my board and I said, "Look, I want to start this speakers bureau. If you give me $25,000, I promise I can get the revenue to maintain it." So my board gave me $25,000. We paid the women $25 an hour while training them. And then I got funding to keep it going.

That's great.

You need to hear from people who have lived experiences in order to have a full understanding of how to serve them.

Do you videotape them and post them anywhere?

Oh yeah, oh yeah. We've got tons of videotapes. Women apply to be part of the speakers bureau. We select ten to fifteen women for each cohort. And over seven weeks we have professionals train them how to speak publicly. Each woman is given a gift every week to honor her contribution, because part of helping people build confidence is continually building their self-esteem and treating them like they're the experts.

And they start feeling like experts. They start acting like experts. When I am offering my expertise, I get paid. So the women that we train get paid, and there isn't one single venue that they attend that isn't paid. And the other thing we've done is that, if you have a venue and you want them to speak and you just don't have the money, we have grant money that will pay them for your event. So I don't ever have to ask a woman to do it for free. Why should these women use their time, talent, skills and knowledge for free?

And these women, have they all experienced homelessness?

It's a mix. There's a mix of women who have been homeless, who have been incarcerated. There's a lot of domestic violence. So it's a mix of experiences, adverse experiences.

How many people do you have on your staff?

Thirty people right now. And we provide a continuum of care. So we start with homeless women and women while they're still incarcerated. And we work with them all the way until they get to permanent housing and everything in between.

I guess fundraising is a constant challenge.

Yes it is. It really is. And I've been pretty successful, but there are so many things that I want to get funding for like research and evaluation. It's hard to get money for those kinds of things. It's hard to get money for new staff. So yeah, I'm constantly fundraising. In August, we have an event for the speakers bureau. The women of the bureau have planned a conference in August and then I have a fundraiser in September, but all of us that are doing nonprofit work struggle with fundraising.

We need funds so we can reach out to people and change their thinking about homelessness and what causes homelessness. The largest percentage of homeless in the United States are children. And I don't think people know that. There are lots of organizations that put out fact sheets, but it doesn't permeate the prevailing narrative. I've been part of so many committees and they're lobbying and advocating and making plans for what we could do if we had the money. But not enough is done to impact the thinking, the narrative.

Are religious groups doing anything in that regard? Are they doing their part to change the thinking and the narrative as you mentioned?

Not enough. I happen to work out of a church, the Lutheran church, which has embraced this as one of their values. And they live out their values through the work that we do. There are some churches that are extremely involved, but in lots of Black communities, the churches aren't doing enough. Let me say that. Not enough to address this issue of homelessness and they are not educated either. They're not. Some of the churches are some of the most divisive, prejudiced institutions I've ever seen.

Hopefully your work and your story will help educate people.

It does. I've worked with churches quite frequently and sometimes I go in and talk to them and people come up later and say, well, I didn't know. You see a lot of that. Then you see some of the thinking shift. I've seen it with my own eyes, but there are lots of churches in communities that aren't knowledgeable about the issue of homelessness and some of them are impoverished themselves, so they don't have the resources to do what needs to be done. But sometimes, like I said, it's not about resources. If we educate the churches, then maybe the communities will come together.

I used to struggle with the church community as a case manager working with the homeless. I had a client once who worked at a post office and when we would do her budget, there was a percentage of her money that was used for tithing. She had to put some money into the church and I'm thinking, can't your church help with the homeless? But she just didn't think that was their obligation, to help her with her homelessness. She gave them a big percentage of her money. Put that into housing, your own personal housing. I realize that I can't influence someone's religious doctrine. And I shouldn't be trying to, but that used to infuriate me.

Can you think of situations where attitudes or opinions changed dramatically in some way?

Well this isn't about homelessness, but I was working in Bucks County [Pennsylvania] which had the highest rate of people in the Aryan Nation in the country. I remember this former Klan member, Cole Cochran. He was a recruiter for the KKK and he had a child that was disabled. It was his Klan brethren that did not accept his child, and it was at that moment that he began to change his views. It took a very personal experience to make him change and his whole life changed. I remember Cole describing the symbolism around what the Klan was all about. He talked about how the youth in that community were being recruited and he became determined to interrupt that recruitment and work against the Klan. It wasn't until he had his own personal experience that he starting making a difference.

An epiphany of sorts?

Yes, that's right.

Are there any questions that I have not asked that I should have asked or any other topics you want to talk about?

Homelessness is so much more than housing, and I'll be honest with you, I've been doing homeless services for the last twenty-five years and I can count on one hand, the number of times I've met someone where housing was the only barrier. So homelessness isn't just about housing. It's so many different elements that make up someone's homelessness. It's about access, about foundation, about education. It's about stable employment. Like I said, I've almost never met a person just needing housing in twenty-five years.

So I wish people would talk more about that because when people hear homelessness, they just think, well, we just need to get them housing. I can't tell you how many people are put in housing but they don't know how to manage housing. They don't know what it means to be a good neighbor. They don't know what it means to be a good tenant. They don't know how to maintain their units. They just haven't had those kinds of experiences. And I find a lot of clients who don't know those things lose the housing after they get it. They need to know how to be a good tenant, budget their money, resolve conflicts, build traditions, all of those things. I've seen so many clients get housing but they don't have any kind of framework in order to maintain it.

I've seen women try to manage their guilt for not being able to give their children what they felt they needed. And it's that guilt that often leads to homelessness again. So you have a woman who's in a program. It's Christmas time and she just felt so bad all year because they were homeless. She takes the rent money and buys all kinds of gifts for her kids but not once realizing that you can't catch up when you don't pay your rent. So you might feel this connection that was lost by buying your children these items, when in reality maintaining the housing is really what they need, not the toys, not the gifts, but as a woman who's feeling guilty about not being able to house her children, she's blinded by this desire to make up for that. And that's the cycle that gets her homeless again. There's so many variables that go into homelessness that need to be unraveled and this idea that it's simplistic is just not reality.

When I first started working with homeless, I could not believe I got paid to help people. I loved what I was doing and still do. I feel so privileged to be able to be a part of helping others and so honored to be able to do it. And that's what keeps me going. That's how I feel about this world. I mean, here I am. I get to help a person change their whole life.

It must be a good feeling.

It is. It's absolutely a privilege to be in a position where I can effect change. I can do something to change someone's circumstances.

I admire you. I congratulate you. And I'm just so thrilled to be able to share your story with other people.

And if there is anything I can do, I want to do it. And I want to make sure that you have access to women who can tell their lived experience.

Thank you very much.

You're very welcome. I told you that I'm always looking for a way to tell the story, educate people and have them join the cause.

It was a pleasure meeting you and talking with you and I look forward to talking to your clients or former clients, and hopefully down the road meeting you in person.

Thank you so much. You have a great day.

You too. Bye now.

GRIMALDI-FRANCESCA SANCHEZ

Grimaldi-Francesca Sanchez is a proud transgender woman who has experienced homelessness and is dedicated to advocating for equity and equality for women and trans people of color. Her work experience includes event management, makeup artistry, business administration and programming.

She is the Founder and Executive Director of Helping Every Rose Bloom (H.E.R.B.), a nonprofit whose mission is to enrich and educate trans youth as well as trans and cis women of color in attaining access to education, housing, professional development and health care.

Grimaldi-Francesca has lived and worked in London, Paris, Rome, Prague and Budapest. She graduated from the University of Tennessee and did graduate work at George Washington University.

Why don't we start with your background. Where were you born and raised?

Well, D.C. is home for me, but I've had the opportunity to live all over the world. D.C. is where I always come back to. It's where I call home. It's where most of my family is and where I've always put down roots no matter what.

And you went to school here in the D.C. area?

Yes, I went to different public schools, middle schools, but I actually wound up graduating at home through American Home School, which was great, and then I went to the University of Tennessee and then GW [George Washington University] for graduate studies in event management.

What was it like in Tennessee?

Even though I felt cultured and worldly, it was definitely a culture shock for me being Black and living in Tennessee. It was in a small town that I actually lived in. I had some experiences. I definitely had some experiences. It made me not want to live in the South ever again truly. However, because of happenstance, I wound up landing in Charlotte, North Carolina, and I fell in love with Charlotte.

So after that, you came back to D.C.?

Yeah.

What kind of work did you do?

Oh, I've done all types of work. My background is in event management, makeup artistry and office administration and programming. In terms of my event background, I've worked everywhere. I've worked at the Spy Museum. I worked at the Smithsonian in the Air and Space Museum and then inside of the Smithsonian. I worked for a company called Amusematte. They did green screen pictures. You could be wearing the Hope Diamond or sitting on dinosaurs, and I eventually became the area manager for that. And then I had the great experience of opening "Bodies, The Exhibition" in Rosslyn, Virginia at the old Newseum building. I was the assistant operations manager for that which was a great experience as well. I've also worked for Chanel, Laura Mercier and Trish McEvoy in terms of my makeup artistry career, most recently, Trish McEvoy. That was my last makeup artist job. I was one of her main artists.

On the administrative side of things, I worked for the Department of Health. I worked at EE2, which is Empowerment Enterprise 2 where I was the program manager and dealt with a lot of their youth programs, opioid programs. They were the fiduciary agents behind the first Trans March on D.C. in September of 2019. That was a great experience to be a part of. So I've done a lot.

It sounds like it.

Those were the main jobs.

Your bio on the website says that you are a proud transgender woman who experienced homelessness and is dedicated to advocating for equity and equality for women and trans people of color.

Yes.

Let's talk about that.

Well, in terms of my advocacy, it's really about educating people and letting them know that trans people are just like anyone else. They want to live healthy lives. They want to secure housing. They want love in their lives just like everyone else. They want jobs. I think that there's such a stigma behind being a trans woman. The perception is that all people in that group are alike, and it's not true.

I just want to show that I'm intelligent, I'm educated, and unfortunately, because of when I decided to transition, my whole life changed and I lost a lot. It's very hard experiencing homelessness. I wasn't brought up going from home to home or seeing poverty on that level, and it was a big shock for me.

How old were you?

Thirty-four. It's been about two years since I was homeless, and that was something I never experienced. It was definitely a shock. I remember my first night at the shelter, just the smells and the uncertainty.

I was working for Trish McEvoy at that time and my main stores were the Bluemercury apothecary stores and I was doing well there. I was a gold member, which meant I sold over $500,000 a year. I always made my benchmarks and was very well liked by my clientele. Then a new district manager for Bluemercury stores came in and immediately just began to pick on me. I was already experiencing a lot of hate and discrimination when I first transitioned in Bluemercury with some of the employees and managers. You would think in the beauty industry that the perception and welcoming would be so much different. It wasn't. I lost a lot of friends and I did not realize the privilege that I had living my life as a gay feminine Black male, but now that I was a Black trans woman, I had lost a lot of privilege and equity that I didn't even know I had. Some clients didn't want to deal with me, and it was very, very stressful making sure I kept up with my goals. One time, a fellow worker pushed me aside, like physically pushed me aside, and one of the managers was there at the time. He said, "Did he just push you?"

People would call and say that what I was wearing was inappropriate for my brand. Mind you, I've never in my life had a problem with someone telling me that the way that I dress is a problem because I'm always dressed impeccably and I always dress to my clients and to the environment that I was in.

I worked in the prestige and luxury beauty work environment for so long. I knew the part and I played it well. One person complained that my heels were too high. We work in beauty and fashion. My heels are too high? They couldn't get me on my work ethic and my sales because that's black and white. So they tried to get me on something else. I am a very strong person but it really beat me down because I was in unfamiliar territory. So eventually, I couldn't take it any longer.

I wound up quitting my job. I was unable to get unemployment and eventually, they came to evict me. I was prepared for it.

So you knew they were coming?

I knew they were coming. Yeah, I definitely knew they were coming. I had asked the judge to give me some time so that I could just get everything out. I really did not want to experience seeing all of my stuff thrown out on the street. It was a very disheartening situation for me because it just seemed like everything was crashing and being taken away from me in one fell swoop. It happened so fast. It all happened really, really fast. It was scary.

So then what happened?

Luckily, one of my friends at that time who lived right next door to me was going out of town and told me I could stay at her place until I got myself together. I didn't want to move back with my mom or my aunts or anyone like that. So I looked for some homeless shelters. I came across Casa Ruby. At that time, they were located on Georgia Avenue and I went there on a Sunday. I sat in the McDonald's across the street for a very long time before I walked in. I had my two rolling suitcases and another two bags with me, and I walked in and that was the very first time I had ever entered a homeless shelter.

I had done community service at food kitchens, but I had never been in a homeless shelter ever in my life. It was probably around one o'clock in the afternoon. I didn't realize that Casa Ruby really only deals with LGBT youth. However, they have services for people over the age of twenty-four. At that time, they had space for six or seven adults to stay in a separate area. You needed to be in there before five o'clock if you're going to get a bed.

Did you get to know any of those young people?

Yes, I did. I actually was able to help some of them. I was seeing some of them just sitting around all day. I would say, "You need to do something." One of them got up and went with me to the D.C. Infrastructure Academy. I got them signed up for that. I'm like, they're going to pay you to get certified. It makes sense. You're here. You need a job. You're going to need employment. You need a skill. You're still very young. You can make a very impactful change in your life and it can start here. So I was able to help some of them. Some were, I found, chronic homeless. I didn't even know that was a thing, chronic homelessness. I learned so much about being homeless. I still had a certain privilege because I never had to be out in the streets in my homelessness. I never had to worry about feeling safe and so many of them do.

When were you able to find work?

I was at the D.C. Infrastructure Academy. I got certified as a flagger because at this time, it's like no one would hire me, not even Chipotle. It was the craziest thing in the world.

What's a flagger?

The construction people. The flaggers. I got certified in flagging. I had my OSHA 10, just anything to keep me busy and try to network so that I could find a job, and they saw that at the shelter. They saw my hunger.

I worked at Krispy Kreme and then at Lyft overnight because I just wanted anything to keep me out of the shelter and to get out of this situation and into some type of housing. So that's what happened.

When did things start to change for you?

Fortunately, because of networking and a friend that I met at the shelter, I got the D.C. Department of Health job and that is what really started to change things a lot for me.

I got that job, but I was still homeless and when the Executive Director found out I was homeless, he was like, "Why didn't you say something?" He actually found me an apartment, which I'm currently still in now.

Let's talk about some your more recent activities, like the Speakers' Bureau.

I speak on advocating for women and trans women because I think it's important that we both have common goals. And I would be remiss if I didn't acknowledge the wonderful and powerful women in my life that raised me, that have guided me and mentored me even when I was living my life as an outwardly gay male. I want to advocate for them too. I want them to know that I'm their partner. I want to be there for them just like they were there for me.

The first big thing I did for my non-profit that I started was a Thanksgiving food drive, and it wasn't just for trans women. It was for women of color, anyone that just needed help, and I was so grateful and honored to be able to share that with my new sisters that I met at the Speakers Bureau.

What kind of reception do you get from your public speaking and other activities?

They say that people make a judgment about you within the first seven seconds, not knowing you, not knowing anything about you, just looking at you. They make an assumption and I always try to make sure that when people see me that they have a positive assumption about me, whatever that may be. I can't control everyone's perception, of course, but I do everything I can to make a positive impression.

The first time I publicly spoke with Speakers Bureau, I discovered that people still classify you. There's some people that I've met through this journey that as they start to discover old parts of my life or the different things I have done in the past, they're like, "Wow, I didn't know that you came from all of that, that you've done so much. Why were you homeless? How could you be homeless?" It's just that it can happen to anyone, and the different ways that it happens, you wouldn't even realize. Literally, from me losing my job, from me transitioning, that's what it all really came down to. I couldn't take it and I'm not a weak-willed person, but I think that they got me at a time when I was very vulnerable because I was newly transitioning and I was still trying to be comfortable in myself and be strong.

I know that I also have a certain amount of privilege, and I acknowledge that. Because of the way that I present myself, and because of my educational background and how I was raised, I have a certain amount of privilege and way of understanding how to approach certain environments and deal with certain types of people. A lot of other trans women don't have that advantage. So I don't experience a lot of hate when I go into new areas. The perception of people wanting to help me is overwhelming at times. People really want to see me succeed and that is very comforting to know.

In most environments, I am very welcome. Right now, I'm in an IT program where I'm the only trans person there and they know that I'm trans. It's not a big deal. It's like I'm just one of the girls in class. We're here to do a job and we know we do it very well.

There are so many issues to deal with being a trans woman facing homelessness. There aren't a lot of trans-only shelters especially in this area. So some of the women might be placed at a male shelter and that presents a challenge, or the women's shelter where the women may not even want them near, so that presents yet another challenge. Chronic homelessness, rampant drug abuse, survival sex work amongst youth, it's very,

very sad. We seem to be so callous as a nation. I think about all the things that we do for other countries, and the amount of things that still need to be done here and it breaks my heart. It truly breaks my heart.

You talked about misperceptions of homelessness. What's the nature of it? Why does it exist and what have you done successfully to change people's perceptions?

I think that it's a thing that's just ingrained into our culture. We think of stereotypical homelessness as either a person that is a drug user, abuses alcohol, is uneducated or may live a life of crime, and that's why they're homeless. What they don't really understand is that a lot of people simply lost some support from the loving network that they needed. For example, they may not be getting proper care for their mental health, like our veterans suffering from PTSD.

Then you have a woman living with her sister in their living room with her four kids. She's homeless. She does not have a place of her own. Yeah, she has shelter, but she's truly homeless. I was thankful that I was able to even get this place because of the eviction. Then as I started to rebuild my life, it's like "Okay, how do I deal with this and that and then find another safe place for me to live?" So you're battling against all of that and when you don't have the willpower, sometimes you end up homeless again because you didn't have the necessary support that you needed.

I don't like it when people say, "I'm not giving them any money because they're going to go buy drugs." I don't want to hear that. If you're going to give them the money, you're giving it because of your heart. Someone asked you for it. We need to stop assuming that everyone is going to live the same and be the same. We have to stop doing that because people end up homeless for so many different reasons. You talk about what do I do to combat that ignorance. One of my friends was saying, "Well, why does a homeless person need a cell phone?" Well, first and foremost, because we live in a technology world and if they are actively trying to find employment, they need a phone. They need to be able to access email to apply for some of these jobs. It's a basic right. They panhandle or do whatever they need to survive, and then they want to go out and buy an iPhone, that's their choice, just like it's your choice to go buy a Chanel bag. You might just have more equity to be able to do things and maneuver whereas they don't. So how dare you say that because they're homeless they don't need a cell phone.

When you talk to people, do they come around?

Yeah, they do, they do, because I know how to really talk to a lot of different people on their levels and tell them what they need to hear and how they need to hear it.

When you're talking to these people, do they know that you experienced homelessness?

I was talking to a close friend who just found out that I had been homeless. I was telling her about our interview. I was like, "I'm getting ready. I have to make sure that I'm getting home to get to this interview," and she asked what it was about. I said, "It's about the time when I was homeless and how I dealt with that." She was dumbfounded. I want people to know and help them understand more about homelessness. I want them to know about my being homeless and try to tell them about how to deal with another homeless person, or tell them my opinion on how they're reacting to it.

I have seen the way that people talk to someone that's homeless on the street and it's despicable. It's just despicable that we treat another human being like that, period, whether they're homeless or not because my thought is, if you treated that person like that on the street, that's part of your character. That's an ingrained part of your character. That's not just because this person might be offensive to you. That's a part of who you are.

We don't need to pass judgment. We need to be offering mental health and other services to these individuals. We need to get to the core reason of why you are homeless and then what kind of care and services you need. Many people did not have financial training or strategy. Let them learn how to budget. There's a lot of intersectionality with homelessness and the probation system and all these different things. It's like we want these people to come out reformed and to be great citizens, but we're not doing anything to truly help. It's like go out and get a job, but make sure that you're back by the three o'clock deadline so that you can check into your bed.

I remember there was a curfew at the men's shelter. Did you have a curfew?

I would literally have to stop what I was doing. First, you got to get up at the crack of dawn and get out there. Then you got to come back before a certain time. And if you wanted to go out at night, that's a problem. But I remember one person that worked at the shelter, she was so sweet. She would allow me to a stay at a friend's apartment on the weekends because she saw the type of person I was and she was like, "So you could just take a regular shower and keep working." Other people didn't care. It's like, "Get up, do this, make sure you're back here by three o'clock."

I had to talk to the caseworkers at the men's shelter and explain to them that some of the shifts were three to eleven so they should make exceptions for these guys because that's the only job they could find.

Yeah, right. It's not fair. I had a caseworker but I really needed her to just give me some transportation tokens when I needed them so I could get to work and back.

The problem with some of the guys at my shelter was that they didn't want to tell the caseworker a lot of things. I had one guy who was a veteran, really smart guy, spoke four languages. But the caseworker didn't understand that he had some issues. One was PTSD and I think he was reluctant to talk to her about it.

Got you. When I spoke with the D.C. Police Reform Commission, that was one of the things I talked about, that a lot of these case managers need to go through peer training and mental health training so that they can identify issues and know how to deal with them. Everyone doesn't need a cookie-cutter solution. You can't truly help a person unless you understand that person and what challenges he or she is having. It could be education. It could be because they need financial training. It's a litany of things and programs that they may need help in.

What kind of programs did you have at your shelter?

I was amazed. There were no programs per se at the shelter. A lot of the young people at the shelter needed more help and they just weren't getting it. They needed lots of specialized attention, and I don't know if the case managers were just overworked or they just didn't have the mental or emotional capacity necessary to deal with a lot of different individuals and their problems. But again, you're dealing in social work. You're dealing in public health. You need to know how to do those things.

Many people think that housing is the solution, that if a person is homeless, man or woman, that you just get them off the street and put them in an apartment and everything's going to be okay. What's wrong with that kind of thinking?

That's where the aftercare services come in. Yes, housing is very key. Some of these programs that I was trying to sign up for to get into housing while being in the shelter want you to be in school, get a job, do all these things, plus come and meet in person to do whatever you got to do for their checkoff list of things that need to be met. But it may not necessarily work for the person. How can you expect a person to do all that stuff? That's just crazy. So you get them the housing, but then you need to keep them housed. So what then do you need? Okay, your health, because you can't be sick and going to work. Now you have a safe place to be, but you can't be sick. Let's get your health together, whatever that may be, mental or physical or both. We need to start making sure that we take care of our community. We have to. So health should be first on the list.

Okay, we got you housed. You got your mental health together because mental health can stop a lot of people from even wanting to work because of their phobias, the discrimination that they've gone through, PTSD, whatever. So you need to take care of that. Okay, we got that all straight. Now a job and/or job training. Everyone should be certified at this point in something. Certification is where it's at. You don't have to have a standard degree anymore. That's why

I've started my IT journey because that's going to be ever evolving. It's going to make sure that I can set myself up in the long run for sustainable income so that as I get older, I know that I'm protected and that I have something to fall back on. So those are things that are very, very important. You can't just house people and then do nothing else. That's crazy. They're going to eventually have the same challenges and issues if you never tried to fix them.

If you were to get a grant for your non-profit, a substantial multi-million dollar grant, what would you do with it?

I would buy an apartment building. I would buy one of these buildings that truly have been for a year and a half vacant that no one was in, these big skyscrapers. My friends and I have talked about this. So this is a perfect question. I would buy a big apartment building, and it could have been former offices or whatever, and I would turn those each into different little apartments for each person, and you would have your common areas. It would be like a dorm almost. You know how dorms are? You have a shared kitchen space. You have a shared place where you can take showers. Then the families, they could have a bathroom in their apartment area.

Then on one of the floors, it would have services -- mental health, employment training, workforce development, professional development and a studio. You want to put money into programming and stuff. Put money into showing people how to truly make a living for themselves. That's what I would do with it.

I know there are buildings like that in D.C.

144

Absolutely. And there's also the little tiny home villages. They definitely should do that. If I did have the opportunity to get another lump sum of money, I would build a little tiny house village for trans women, like in the outskirts of Maryland or somewhere like that. But you have to think about things like transportation. Okay, you've housed them, but now how are they going to get to where they need to go?

Have you seen what they're doing with these forty-foot shipping containers?

Yes, I love that. I've seen those shipping containers. I saw that in California and Nevada. They've made them into homes and businesses.

You've talked a lot about the importance of health care. I'm going to read you something and get your reaction.

Okay.

The Center for American Progress report found that nearly half of transgender people and sixty-eight percent of transgender people of color reported having experienced mistreatment at the hands of a medical provider, including refusal of care and verbal or physical abuse. This was in 2019.

Yeah, so you're hitting on some really good questions, Deno. I actually had this conversation with my doctor about three weeks ago. I go to Whitman Walker for my healthcare, dentist, my primary care, for my hormones, everything. That's where I go and my experience, come to find out, is not the experience of a lot of trans women in the area, and I did not know that. I have such a great team of doctors that I've never felt anything but compassion and empathy to help me and my transition goals and to be successful. But a lot of what you read goes on. It's so crazy that to this day some doctors are still are not comfortable dealing with transgender patients. You practice medicine. You're about healing and trying to heal people in their time of need.

I was very disheartened to hear that a lot of my sisters had gone through so many different mistreatments. It's not an experience that I can speak to personally because I have not had that happen to me. Even when I've had to go to the ER, I've always made sure that no one ever misgendered me. I made sure that I did everything to try to combat those types of situations. I made sure of that. But for a lot of people, it's just so sad that you're going somewhere and you're sick and you're trying to get help, but then you still have to deal with discrimination. It's very sad, and those are the people that you want to trust. And as a result, suicide is rampant and real.

Well it's been a real pleasure meeting you and talking to you and learning from you.

Thank you, Deno.

Keep up the good work.

Thank you so much, Deno.

You take care.

You too.

Bye now.

Bye.

AARON HOWE

Aaron is a Ph.D. candidate in anthropology at American University in Washington, D.C. He earned a B.S. degree in anthropology with a minor in archaeology and history at Grand Valley State University and an M.A. in anthropology at Western Michigan University.

For his doctoral dissertation, he is conducting an ethnography of homeless encampments in the District of Columbia. Aaron believes it is crucial that anthropologists become more involved with homelessness policy.

Aaron is the co-founder of Remora House, an organization that provides supplies and assistance to individuals living in homeless camps and shelters in the D.C. area.

Your dissertation on the ethnography of homeless encampments, when do you plan to complete it?

I'm currently trying to write it up which, unfortunately because of COVID, I don't have access to my university. I don't have as much access to my advisors. I don't have reading groups like I normally would, so the writing is slow and then all the work I've been doing with Remora House has taken up a lot of my time. So it's coming along. It should be done in about a year.

I've come across some parallels with your work. For example, Tracy Kidder's book on Paul Farmer, the medical anthropologist.

Oh yeah, I've read that book.

You've talked about the anthropology of homelessness. Could you elaborate on that for me?

Farmer figured out that the mother of the group or the clan would be given the medicine and she would distribute it to the people, instead of following the Western model where maybe you have a clinic or the doctors go around. But by going to the mothers of the clan, Farmer was able to get the medicine actually distributed to people. And he learned that through anthropology. So with anthropology and ethnography, we just go out and talk to people. That's a big thing. And we don't just talk to people, we also try to participate in their daily lives and really understand, not just what homelessness or life is about, but what are some of the mundane things you wouldn't really think about.

I talk a lot about physical and emotional stress from homelessness. I spent a lot of time going to the homeless encampment engagements, what D.C. calls the cleanups.

You've been to several dozen.

Yeah, man. I went to many. During my dissertation, I was going twice a week, every week for a year. Sometimes people would miss the cleanup signs and I would always hear from the city like, "Oh, we gave them a two-week warning. The signs are up." But from an anthropological perspective, it was very clear that yeah, those signs are up, they do see them, but the streets are full of signs, parking signs. So one more sign, they don't always notice them. And then they're up for two weeks, so they notice it once. And then, they don't have an iPhone app calendar to plug that into. And so the two weeks comes and that just kind of slips their mind. It's a very serious slip-up because they can end up losing their property and their belongings and stuff.

When did you first become interested in homelessness?

I'm doing my Ph.D. now. I did both my undergrad and my master's in anthropology with a focus in archaeology. I actually went out and I dug dirt, traditional archaeology. My focus has always been migrant labor, company towns. So my master's focused on logging in Michigan where I'm from. I looked at how they constructed homes and how homes were used in different ways to reproduce daily life. And then how some of that was used by the logging company, because if you think of logging, they're constantly on the move. You had boarding house style housing and the typical way we think of loggers is single men out in the woods. But I worked specifically with families out in the woods.

So from that, I came to American University to do archaeology. I tried to do archeology in D.C. It didn't work out and as I was looking for sites, I actually came upon the homeless camps in D.C. and just quickly transitioned to doing that. Also, I worked with a few other very prominent anthropologists of homelessness scholars in my master's program. That kind of helped me transition from doing archeology to doing ethnography.

What have you learned so far?

I think on the most large scale, there's no silver bullet solution to ending homelessness. One of the misconceptions I had going into this work was that all homeless shelters should be low barrier. Everyone should be able to get a room if they want a room, no matter what they do, what type of personality they have, what substances they might use. I learned pretty quickly that some people actually need high barrier shelters.

Some women in particular, some older women in particular don't want to be around like, drug users, or if they're trying to get clean themselves, they don't want to be around that stuff. There should be a space for them.

And then there's the tiny house thing, more in the west coast, but in different types of sheltering options. I saw row single room occupancies, permanent supportive housing, rapid rehousing, more and more because there's a lot of pushback against the tiny house thing.

You mean like a NIMBY pushback?

Yes, there is that, but what I mean is from advocates, homeless advocates.

Why is that?

They're saying that's not dignified housing. We should give them full housing, not tiny houses, which I also understand, but then at the same time, some people do very well in tiny homes. I hear from so many homeless people that they want a tiny home. But then other people are like, "I'm not going to fit in a tiny home." So again, it's not a homogeneous group and we need this variety of housing solutions. And then the same with the communal living situations. I saw rows where you have your own room and maybe your own bathroom, but a shared kitchen, maybe a shared bathroom too. Also works very well for some people, not for others.

Yeah, I saw an interesting tiny house village in Portland.

Right. I think it's called Dignity Village.

In an article you wrote a couple of years ago, you said, "Clean-ups from what I observed, are not for the health and safety of all D.C. residents. Instead, they are violent." You touched on this briefly and I know that you and one of your colleagues have gone around with replacement tents and supplies and toothbrushes and so forth. It breaks my heart when I read about this. Tell me what you have seen and what it's actually like for these people.

There's been a lot of changes since I wrote that piece. It was pre-COVID. There's a different person in charge of the cleanups now. And now we're actually going through another transition because her position was policy analyst, but she was the on-the-ground person that did the engagements, the cleanups. And when I started, they were just transitioning to a new person and for most of my research, I was with one of those policy analysts. And then once COVID hit, it was actually like three or four months before that the person I was used to working with quit and they got a new one and then all through COVID we had the same one. D.C. followed the CDC guidelines pretty well, decently well about not clearing encampments. So they did what's called trash only engagements.

People used to have to move, and once again, they have to move all their stuff so the city could do their cleanup and then move it back when they were done. During trash only, the city would just come by and the homeless residents would make piles or areas of trash, and then they would pick up that trash. But the COVID policy analysts actually recently just quit as well, because D.C.'s about to escalate their engagements. Do you know about the K Street underpass at all?

I've seen it.

Yeah, it's where I did most of my work and they made it a tent-free zone or a pedestrian passageway is what they call it. And so they used an anti-homeless law to clear out forty tents from an underpass, and now there's no tents there. This was January 2020, right before COVID and the main two other underpasses on M and L Streets, where about sixty people live is about to also be made another tent-free zone. It's still in the works what's going to happen, but it's going to be made another pedestrian passageway in some way, shape or form. They are clearing it. D.C. says that the engagements were for the health and safety of all D.C. residents, including those experiencing homelessness. And to a point it's true, right? Safe, clean spaces are important for everybody. But this goes back to the time thing I was talking about earlier - when you miss one of those cleanups or engagements, you lose all your stuff.

That doesn't only hurt individual homeless people, but hurts the housing system at large because the homeless population loses trust in the people that are supposed to be providing services to get them into housing. What if someone that came and threw away your tent home and the next day tried to come get you on a list to get you into actual housing? You're not going to trust that person anymore and it leads to what the industry calls a service resistance or home resistance. In reality, people aren't resistant to homes or services, they're resistant to the constant violence and harassment they face from the same people.

How were you accepted among the people in the encampments?

It's a heterogeneous community; it's not homogeneous. Going through these encampments, I didn't go and just watch. I actually helped people move their stuff. In anthropology, we talk about access and entrance into communities. That was a huge access point for me. I got a lot of solidarity from people, a lot of trust. But I was also out there almost every day. One time somebody had court in the morning and they had to pay their court fee to get their records. They had to be there at 8:00 a.m. And I was like, "I'll show up at 6:40, I'll take care of the twenty dollars, and I'll make sure you can access court and get your probation things squared away." And they were like, "Oh, okay." And then I showed up at 6:40 in the morning with the money and waited for him. His face just lit up when he saw me. So things like that where you show solidarity got me a lot of recognition and acceptance pretty quickly.

And then also just not being one of the normal actors or people they're used to seeing. I never asked for their name, their social security number. I didn't pry about addiction or mental health. A lot of times, I would just sit and talk for an hour or two hours, whatever about whatever. Still, there were for sure people who didn't like me though. I didn't have full access or complete trust.

Why didn't they like you?

I don't know, but I guess it could be multiple reasons. One, I'm a White boy in a gentrifying area. And that was actually something that was brought up a lot. And a lot of people apologize to me when they talk about White people or Caucasians. Sometimes I would get the nod like, oh, but not like you, and then talk about the other people in the high-rises, the people that hold their nose when they walk through the encampment or walk through the road instead of walking by the tents and things like that.

Tell me about Remora House. What are some of your activities? What do you hope to achieve in the future?

Remora House was started by me and my partner, Shannon. We started right after COVID. I was trying to organize, get hand sanitizer, wipes, things like that to the camps and to some of the shelters in D.C. At that point, we were just pretty much begging people on Facebook and Twitter. That was some of our first, very first supply drops that we got. So that was kind of how we started as a group. And then from that, we just slowly started expanding. I would say our main scope and what we do is we provide supplies for the camps in D.C. We do a little bit of work in the shelters. We do a little bit of work recently with getting people supplies after they get their housing vouchers.

Does the name Remora have any significance?

Remora is a fish. They're little sucker fish that attach to sharks and clean off the bad bacteria from sharks. And then the sharks keep predators away from the small Remora fish.

A symbiotic relationship?

Yeah, it's a mutual relationship in general. And we consider ourselves a mutual aid group. Remora House. We thought it sounded nice.

Are you a 501(c)(3)?

We're a 501(c)(4) currently. We got that maybe six months ago but we're thinking about switching to C3. We consider ourselves mutual aid, which is the trend right now. But we're also pretty far left politically. We mainly do supplies for unhoused and recently unhoused people in particular. And then we do the engagement camp defense and organization around that, largely getting volunteers to come and help people move stuff, which is actually like a trend that we're seeing in a lot of cities across the United States with camps in general.

And then we do a lot of one-on-one support. So a lot of people have our phone numbers. And currently, we're trying to help somebody get baby stuff. His girlfriend's having a baby so we're trying to get baby stuff for them.

Two weeks ago we helped organize a vigil for a man who passed at one of the camps where we work.

We do fundraising for various things people need. Once a week, Shannon and I go to the camps with our carts and supplies and we just kind of walk around the camps and hand them out as needed. And then we do the one-on-one support as well.

Shannon's currently at Wal-Mart buying pants, shirts, a few tents, gas canisters for cooking, things that people specifically requested, including sizes, what colors they want and stuff like that. And we'll hand those out Saturday.

Tell me about your Metro card distribution.

The D.C. department in charge of revamping Metro ridership post-pandemic is trying to get people to ride the Metro again. They sent us and a few other groups eighty Metro cards, ten dollars each. And we talked them into actually giving us a hundred Metro cards a month with twenty dollars each on them. It's kind of a weird relationship we have with them, but I think we're going to be getting a regular supply from the city, which is big. A lot of people use the bus and the Metro regularly.

Where does your funding come from?

One hundred percent of our funding comes from social media, small donations. We got a five-hundred-dollar donation the other day which is, I think, the biggest donation we ever got. And it's one of the reasons we're thinking of becoming a C3. We're trying to get grants and we found a few we can get as a C4, but as a C3, more people are willing to give us grants.

What questions that I'm not asking should I be asking?

I don't know. I mean, there's so much.

What can we do to make people more aware of homelessness?

I have both a pessimistic and an optimistic answer to that question. My knowledge and interests are very D.C. focused. I know D.C. is a little different than other areas, and so the pessimistic part is, I think homelessness is becoming a more visible and glaring issue already. We need to change the discourse around street homelessness away from criminalization or clean up or harassment to one of a humane solution, to actually funding services that we know work. We know permanent supportive housing with wraparound services works. We also know it's expensive, but we know it works. And we know criminalization, cleanups, et cetera, only push the problem around to different places.

NIMBYs can be very happy because it's not in their park anymore. But that doesn't actually solve anything long-term or for the individuals involved. So I don't know if I have a great optimistic answer to how can we change that narrative, but I've been doing this work for about three years and I've seen a huge change from the previous year to this year. The rise in mutual aid groups after COVID and a lot more young people becoming active in feeding, offering supplies, et cetera, to the camps has grown dramatically.

A while ago, when I was doing my research, it was pretty much me, the larger nonprofits and church groups. Now you've got scores of young liberals and progressives out there. And I think if we can keep that momentum going, I think it's going to be a huge turning point because young people are a huge force in the country writ large, and they have the ability to press for these changes in a way that we weren't able to.

We're willing to take risks. If Remora House collapses under its own weight, we'll just rise up again as something else. We're not tied to grantors. It's one thing that does worry us about some grants with conditions that don't let us do certain things. We're super concerned about some of the camp removals that are coming up in D.C.

Tell me about these camp removals.

In 2015, D.C. had its first major camp removal since probably the 1980s. It was by the Watergate hotel under the Whitehurst Freeway. And they built a hundred-thousand-dollar fence around it. It just pushed people to further parts of the city. Since then, I know two other permanent evictions like that. There's the K Street one in 2020 and 2021, and there's three or four more coming up. So D.C. is criminalizing homelessness at a higher rate. It's something that worries me a lot. And especially since homelessness is on the rise.

What are your plans after you get your doctorate?

I don't know. When I started the Ph.D., my hope was to teach at the college level. I teach now and I've taught in the past. But the prospects for higher education teaching is very low. It's a very tough job market and competitive, and you have to write and write and write, and I don't want to just write and write and write.

You want to do and do and do.

Yes, I want to do. There is room and space for, we call them engaged anthropologists. Some people call them activist anthropologists. There is room for that. In academia, it's still very cutthroat. I no longer want to do that. I think more and more, especially after starting Remora, I want to continue doing a non-profit role in D.C. with homelessness. Working with some other people who do that work in order to learn more would probably be useful because I know I've made a lot of mistakes already in this past year. But yeah, I don't have set in stone plans anymore.

What would be the first three things you would do if you got a substantial grant with no strings attached?

One of the things I hear over and over again is kind of like an SRO style shelter housing. The people I work with call it hotel housing.

What does SRO mean?

SRO – single room occupancy. And they were really popular like pre-1970s. Pretty neo-liberal, urban renewal. A lot of city centers had these very cheap lodgings. In the twenties, they were sometimes called flop houses or things like that, where you could get one night to one month of stay for very cheap. You had your own room and then shared facilities - shared kitchen, shared bathroom maybe. I think some shelter options like that would be great. I think there needs to be housing options outside of the voucher program to get people who are not eligible for the housing voucher program back on board.

So one of my biggest critiques of the housing first approach and permanent supportive housing we have is that in order to be eligible to get a federal housing voucher, to get a local house paid for by the government, you need to be chronically homeless, which means homeless for one year or more, or homeless four times in the past three years. One of the problems is, the condition of homelessness is very brutal. So being homeless for one year gets a lot of those stereotypes of homelessness going. A lot of people get mental health issues in that one year or get addicted to substances in that one year. I would like to push for that to be changed, so we don't just focus on housing the chronically homeless, we focus on housing writ large.

Aaron, I really do appreciate this and I wish you all the luck in the world with your dissertation and the good work you're doing.

Yeah, thank you.

It was nice meeting you.

Nice meeting you too.

ANDRE WYCHE

Andre is a husband, father and thirteen-year Air Force Veteran. He has been in combat operations seven times, had flight status on four different types of cargo aircraft, five different helicopters and was a crew chief on a helicopter. He has lived abroad in Guam, Japan, Korea and the Philippines.

Andre holds a Bachelor's Degree in Accounting from the University of Maryland, has worked in the tech sector, served as a public school teacher and is a polyglot who speaks five languages with varying degrees of fluency. He has experienced periods of homelessness.

Andre, what I hope to do with this book is to share stories from people who have experienced homelessness, and from people working to end homelessness. So why don't we start. Where did you grow up?

Well, my dad was career military Air Force, so we traveled around quite a bit. My two older sisters were born in Paris, France. I was born right here in Hampton, Virginia, but then we went all over the Far East. We started with Hawaii, then Guam, Japan, Korea, Philippines, and then my dad had an opportunity to get stationed at Andrews Air Force Base. So we moved to Maryland and that's pretty much where I went through the last part of junior high, high school, and then enrolled at PG Community College. And then I switched over to the University of Maryland.

So right about '79, '80, '81, that's when all the crack and all the drugs were coming into primarily the east coast. And even as a teenager, I saw the handwriting on the wall. So I knew I didn't want to stay in the area. My dad was on the tail end of his Air Force career, and I know he didn't want to stay in this area. So I joined the Air Force myself. That was my breakaway to not only get away from the area that was getting ready to get entrenched with a heavy drug flow and all the violence that followed behind it. But also it allowed me to finish my education and get my bachelor's degree.

So that was the situation, but I didn't mean to add more than what you asked for.

No, I appreciate that because it gives me an understanding of your background. You were exposed to a lot of different cultures all over the world. That's an education in and of itself. And so what did you study in college?

I really liked to cook and I wanted to be in culinary arts or an executive chef. My thing coming out of school was, I was going to be executive chef and be on a cruise ship. So I was going to be able to travel and cook. But by the time I got to my junior year, they had changed the requirements, and I was like, well, I don't want to spend that much time in school. And then when I looked at my credit hours and looked at the matchup of other degrees that I could get without wasting my time, I saw that I could get an accounting degree.

So then you switched majors?

I did. And the only day off I had was Sunday. I had daytime classes, Monday, Wednesday and Friday, then evening classes, Tuesday, Thursday and Saturday. And I had jobs to flex for that whole six-day schedule.

And then one day, this lady at the school, if she was alive today I would kiss her because the way she broke it down to me, she gave me all the information I needed to make the best choices. A lot of times you talk to people and it's like, they only give you part of the roadmap and they don't tell you where all the potholes are.

What did she tell you?

Basically she said, if you can get stationed at Yokota Air Base in Japan, where Maryland taught courses, and have a two-year tour and get a job that allows you to stay there, you could get your degree in the two-year timeframe or even less.

And I'm not trying to get all religious here, but I prayed about it. My dad did a combat tour in Vietnam in '66 and '68, so my mom was just out for any of her children joining the military. And I knew if I could sell it to my dad, I could get him to sell it to mom.

Did you sell it?

Yes. My mom was upset but things started to fall together. Long story short, I got stationed at Yokota Air Base, Japan.

This was a sweet setup back then. The Air Force Education Program at that particular time, if you made an A in your course, the Air Force paid for ninety percent. If you made a B in your course, they paid for eighty percent. If you made a C, they paid for seventy percent. Less than that, they didn't pay for anything. I always either made either A's or B's, so I got my degree. Maryland mailed it to me to in Japan. And then it was Australia, New Zealand, Germany, Thailand, Panama, Desert Storm. I got hurt during Desert Storm. I pretty much tore up my left knee and my right shoulder.

And after your discharge, what then?

Marriage, two children. But it took me about two years after I got out of the military to adjust. And here's the thing, I've been in combat operations seven times. I have flight status on four different types of cargo aircraft for the Air Force, five different helicopters. I was a crew chief on a helicopter. I got a bachelor's degree and an associate's degree, and at the time, not fluently, but I learned to speak five different foreign languages thanks to the military and Berlitz.

My credit profile was good. But I couldn't find a job anywhere. I got out of the military and I was having problems big time.

As I said, my dad was in the Air Force and I have an uncle that was in the Air Force. They're military-minded, so they could understand it. But my cousins, my sisters, I couldn't explain that to them. And even if I did, they wouldn't believe me. So I just kept my mouth shut.

What kind of work did you find?

I was working at one factory making suntan lotion during the day, and then at night, I was making Stove Top stuffing. And the thing about that is, when those factory jobs have a slowdown, they get rid of the temp workers first before they get rid of their full-time staff. So those jobs lasted about six months, and then I went to work at a Playtex Bra factory from seven in the morning until seven at night. Then I went to work at Perdue, cleaning up chicken crap. And the whole time, I had to dumb down my resume. I didn't mention that I had a bachelor's degree. I didn't mention that I had an honorable discharge.

Because they would think you were overqualified or something?

Yeah.

Let me just explore this for a second, because some of the vets I've met at my shelter are telling me almost the exact same story. They had a strong work ethic, management ability, discipline, the ability to adapt, some like you spoke several languages, and somehow, American employers couldn't appreciate that type of skill set and training. So what can we do to make American employers understand that hiring veterans would be in their absolute best interest? Any ideas?

A civilian or regular employer would have to see the base core of what a veteran would give them. They know how to dress properly. They know how to be timely for meetings and formations. They know how to listen to instruction and direction and complete tasks, goals, and objectives. And then, last, but not least, you have a person that if something goes a little crooked, they won't fly off the handle, lose their composure, lose their cool. They will handle a particular situation and try to straighten it out as best as possible.

Then there's the VA. It needs to run public service announcements and say, "Hey, guess what, American public? We've put these men and women in harm's way for our country. Now they need an opportunity to be able to come back and have some semblance of life."

When did you first experience homelessness?

My wife and I divorced. I didn't have my own place, so I moved back with my mom, which pretty much kept me off the streets. That was my first time ever being in that situation. So, dealing with that situation, that really stripped me down to nothing, and I do mean absolutely nothing. I told my mom, I said, "Give me sixty days. I'll have everything in order."

I had a little bit of money saved, and I saw that the D.C. police force was hiring, so I went there and they had the physical test. You had to sign the waiver just in case you had a heart attack on them, and I passed the test with the best times. And then, one of the people there says, "Have you ever shot a gun?" I said, "Yeah, from a revolver to a sniper. And then, I realized, "Do I really want to be a police officer?" I decided, eh, maybe not.

So I ended up becoming a school teacher with the D.C. Public School system at Ballou High School in Southeast D.C. At that time, there was so much corruption going on. You know you're supposed to get a paycheck every two weeks? I'd get two paychecks this month, one paycheck the next. Two paychecks the month after that because they were mismanaging the money and just floating the shell game to make sure everybody got paid. I mean, it was really that bad. You can Google that. Look at the D.C. Public School system corruption in 1996. It was terrible. So I moved into a two bedroom apartment and started doing tech work and seeing the stepping stones in the lily pad. This was my chance to get out of my situation.

Transitional and permanent housing is critical for people experiencing homelessness. Any thoughts?

You got buildings sitting out here that are stone empty. So let's rework those buildings into actual living spaces, with the tie-in to educate people in that same building where they live. First of all, we're going to get you in there. You're going to learn to take care of yourself. We're going to get you rid of those bad habits and teach you manners and self-respect. And that proliferates out to the other people you live next to.

A homeless person is often under a lot of stress, especially when they don't know when they're going to eat, where they're going to sleep, where they're going to take a bath, if they have supplies to clean themselves up. You need toothpaste, toothbrush, bar soap, towel and washcloth. So Tuesday, Thursday and Saturday, you're going to class just to be a better person. Monday, Wednesday and Friday, you're picking up trash or cleaning up cigarette butts if you see them out in front of where you live.

So the government doesn't have to pay as much as they would if that person remains homeless. Some people commit crimes just to be in jail. They just want to be in jail to have somewhere to stay. So you cut that out. You reduce the crime in a neighborhood because now you got a person that has a place to stay. They're not just so-called loitering. Then you got an area where a person can in turn, say, "Okay, wow, I got a place that I can safely and securely not only keep myself, but I can keep what little bit I have in life without it being stolen, me being molested, trampled on and just basically disrespected."

Are you having any success communicating this to employers and businesses in Fairfax County? Are they being receptive?

I don't even talk to anybody anymore. You're the first person I've talked to, other than the few family members I have left and the few military guys I served with in the military. Seriously, you're the first man I've spoken to in, I would say probably about a year, year and a half. I'm to the point now, I'm just so disgusted with people that I hardly even talk to anybody anymore.

I hear you.

My wife talks to other people. She does what she does. And to me, she's Wonder Woman.

I enjoyed my interview with her. She really is amazing.

So I'll support Wonder Woman. I'll be the rest of the Justice League, but behind closed doors. I'm at the point now in my life with the kids here in the house with us, I want to show them a good example, and I really don't have the inkling or the time to talk to anybody. At the end of the day, I've noticed in my life there's two types of people -- those talking about doing it and those that are actually doing it. And then people like yourself. The mere fact that you want to put together a book and disseminate information and educate people, that's a lovely and wonderful thing.

Thank you Andre. So tell me, how long did you actually experience homelessness?

When I had gotten out of the Air Force and got divorced, that was the first time. I was actually homeless and I finally knuckled down and reached out to my mom like I was telling you. My parents were divorced and I didn't even tell my dad. I didn't talk to any of my sisters or anything. After that, I got a job but the company went out of business. Then I was staying in different hotels. I was homeless. So, for about three months, I was staying in different hotels until I got my act together, and then I was staying in a one bedroom apartment on my own. And then my mom got pancreatic cancer.

That sounds overwhelming.

I mean, I dealt with it. I didn't like it, but I dealt with it.

Were you suffering from any PTSD from overseas, any issues there?

Yeah. My wife says I still do. So for all the grandeur that they talk about, on one hand, they say they want to help you out, but when you're in the Special Forces, Special Operations community, once you get that flag on your record that someone talked to you from psych, you're pretty much persona non grata. I said to myself, right about 2007, 2008, that I had to get my game, get my act in order, wrap it up a little bit tighter than what it was. I said I'm no good to myself or anybody else if I don't get my act in order. I was just basically really dealing with certain triggers that still even get to me. It was even worse back then, so I had to get my act in order.

It looks like you did a pretty job of that. A recent study showed that on average, it costs about $65,000 a year per person experiencing homelessness in this country, and around $15,000 a year to find permanent housing for that person. So it appears to be cheaper to house people than to have them be homeless. Any thoughts about that?

The homeless situation in this country, that just irritates me. Prime example, right down the street in Alexandria, Virginia, near the Landmark Mall, a premier mall back in the late '70s, mid '80s. And then, it just dropped off with the creation of Amazon. Everybody decided to do a whole bunch of mail order. And then, the demographics changed. A lot of the big money people that lived in that area of Alexandria moved out, so you had that big, empty mall space and homeless people. And then, what ends up happening is, you get the NIMBY people, not in my back yard.

And it's a situation where, if you don't properly take care of these people that have been shuttered through the system or shuttered through life, they're going to be in your back yard regardless. It's better to have them in the back yard organized, in a safe place, a safe part of society. They don't want to have anything stolen and more than likely, they don't want to steal from anybody. But now, when you put them in a stressful situation where they don't have a clean toothbrush, they might be tempted to shoplift. And then you're going to put somebody in jail? Then what? At Wal-Mart, a toothbrush is $3. So you're going to now mess up their personal record over a $3 toothbrush?

And just one note, before we call it quits on this, from one man to another, just talking to you, I feel a little bit better today, and I just want to say thank you. I appreciate you.

Well the feeling is mutual. I appreciate you talking with me and I look forward to one day when we can visit in person. Thanks again and take care.

You too.

DENIS ELIS

Denis Elis was born in the Ural Mountains area of Russia. He and his family emigrated to the United States when he was fourteen.

Denis had an early interest in computers which led him to study computer science at the University of Maryland and work in jobs that required advanced computer skills. He is a U.S. Army veteran.

Denis has experienced homelessness and was part of a development team exploring the feasibility of building a tiny house village for homeless men in Montgomery County, Maryland.

Denis! How are you?

Doing fine.

Are you working?

Yes and no. I am employed, but I'm not working because if my boss doesn't have work, I don't have work. And because of COVID, he has far less work. I'm supposed to see him tomorrow, but it depends on the weather because I have to drive to D.C. If it snows, we're going to cancel and reschedule for another day.

Are you doing computer work?

I work as a personal assistant for retired Navy JAG. He runs a couple of his own businesses from home, so I kind of assist him with pretty much everything. He's eighty years old, so he's not too computer savvy. I've taught him quite a lot. He's done better, but he's still a bit slow. Sometimes he'll get overwhelmed with work so I have to help him catch up on some of the things he does. He's a great boss. Awesome guy.

You heard what happened to the shelter?

The methane.

Right. They set up a new shelter down the street in an abandoned office building. Not an ideal setup. Trailers outside with bathrooms and showers. But they did get some new computers for the job searching.

That's good.

Why don't we start with your background. Tell me where you grew up? What was family life like? Where did you go to school?

Born in Russia originally. Parents divorced when I was two, but I saw my dad on a regular basis when my parents could stand each other long enough to talk to each other. I would spend the weekend with the dad.

What part of Russia?

It's called Ural Mountains. Spent a lot of time in the country, so I grew up around chickens and pigs. Worked a little bit of farm work. I wasn't poor, so I wasn't asked to do it, but I did it for the fun of it. I was encouraged.

As a kid growing up, you didn't have computers like nowadays, so doing anything outdoors was a lot of fun. Then my mother and I moved here to the United States in '91 on March 27th. I was fourteen. My birthday's on the 29th, so it's like a pretty big deal, these two dates, because they're so close together.

How did you feel about moving to another country?

For some people, they move to the states and they forget about it. For other people, they never forget about it because it's such a big change, such a big leap. Then my mother got married to a really great guy. Unfortunately, the marriage did not work out. My mother married him for a green card. She needed the green card, and as he offered to get married, she agreed to it. But the marriage didn't work out. The main issue was that there was a big age gap. They were a little different too. Personalities were different. He was an attorney, a pilot, a historian. He actually had his own airplane, a private airplane.

I remember you telling me that's how you got interested in aviation.

Right. He also knew quite a lot about World War II history, Egyptian history. Great guy, but at the end of the day, my mother and him, they were different people. They separated. Then she worked for an adoption agency helping American families who can't have kids adopt children from outside the U.S.

What were you interested in growing up? When did you become interested in computers?

Computers started with high school. A buddy of mine, he was into computers. Then another buddy had a computer. At the beginning, I wasn't really interested in computers. It started out as a hobby. To me, it was more like playing video games and surfing the internet or whatever the internet was back then. Right after high school, I went into the Army. I wanted to be a pilot. My mother actually had a meltdown. She blew the metaphorical head gasket because she was scared for me.

She did not want you to join the military?

Right, she did not because she worked as a dentist at a military hospital. She saw the aftermath of the soldiers coming back from Afghanistan. Anyway, I joined the military and my mother for sure was scared.

That was eight years in the Army, interesting experience. But I realized pretty early on that the military wasn't really for me, because as you and I know, sometimes we have to take orders. A soldier has to take orders even if they don't make sense. And if it doesn't make sense, it just goes against our better judgment. We've seen this throughout history. We've seen it in the news when a soldier, a pilot, has to take an order, and then a year or five years down the road he finds out that the people that were killed, they were civilians. They were not enemies. It still happens. Not as often I'm guessing, but probably still happens.

They called me at the end of 2004. The recruiter told me, "Hey, come back. Why don't you rejoin again?" I said, "No, I'm not interested," because I was not interested in that war at all. I didn't want to be part of that war in the Middle East. I'm just glad I didn't go because that war is a complete cluster fuck, excuse my French. It's no end in sight.

And then you went to school. What did you study?

I went to Maryland. I decided to go with computer science because I already liked computers. Working in computers was pretty easy for me. It was fun because it started out as a hobby. I also thought of becoming a psychiatrist and I minored in psychology, but then it was just too much coming into my brain. I couldn't deal with it. What's the word I'm looking for? Analyzing. I started analyzing everything -- my life, my current life, my past life, when I was a kid, my parents, the trees, the buildings. I mean I analyzed how everything affected me, and it just put me into a depression.

And after college, where did you work?

I started with computers, working with companies here and there. But I lost interest. That's when I met you. Do you remember? I started losing interest because I lost interest in the hobby itself, working with computers at home, building computers. I wanted to do something else. Still even years later, after you and I met, I still think about flying, but flying is just not an option anymore for me, even if I had all the money in the world to go to flight school.

When I was homeless, after you and I had met, I actually ended up living in a car. I worked in an Amazon warehouse. Then I hurt my leg. Had to go to physical therapy. Almost eight months of physical therapy for my leg. Then last year, right before the COVID in March, I had two brain strokes.

Oh no.

Yeah, two days apart. I recovered for the most part. I did all the tests, CT scans and everything and they said, "You look fine. Everything looks good."

Were they mild strokes?

Yes, they were mild strokes. There was no long-term damage, but it was still a dampener.

Did it affect your memory?

It did. When I was healing, it did. The memory was pretty bad. Daily tasks were difficult. Sometimes I'd take a clean dish and put it in the refrigerator or take food out of refrigerator and then put it in the cupboard where the clean dishes go.

Are you on medication?

Basically, I have to take aspirin for the rest of my life, small little baby aspirin. It came down to a vein in the back of my neck. It popped and then when it popped, it started creating a clot in the front lobe. Basically, it all comes down to stress, just a lot of stress.

How are you dealing with the stress?

It's still there. It's not as bad as it used to be, but it's still there. That's a whole story of its own too because after my mother passed away, I've been in a legal battle over my mother's house and estate with her latest husband. We're still going at it for almost four years.

I remember you telling me about it.

Right, so it's still ongoing.

When you first experienced homelessness, do you remember how it happened and how you felt?

The first time it happened, I had to walk out of the house. I was living with my mother and her husband. I was taking care of her because she was ill with cancer, her third cancer. My mother and I were never close and her husband, he was a piece of work himself. There was a lot of negativity in that household, negative energy. I was falling into a depression. I had no choice. I just had to walk out. Part of me kind of felt glad that I pulled myself out of that house. But at the same time, I was more frustrated at myself than anything else that I got sucked into this situation, taking care of my mother for ten years. The first time I ended up being homeless, it felt like a pause. It was a pause. It's like taking a long pause on life. It felt like I'm having an abrupt stop to everything that I'm doing.

In my case, I wasn't losing exactly everything, but at the same time, my life just made a complete stop. You kind of get lost. There's no direction. It's almost like having a break up. All of a sudden, your girlfriend just breaks up one day with you for no reason and that's it. It's just over. You're kind of dumbfounded. You don't know what's going on and what's going to happen. I know it's different for everyone because everyone's situation is different, but I kind of chose to be homeless to save myself.

Right before I walked out, I was contemplating killing myself because my mental health was degrading so badly. I bought a handgun. I was going to kill myself. I was going to shoot myself. I almost did. I got drunk twice and I wanted to kill myself both times. I just couldn't do it because I didn't want to die. I wanted to live. I just wanted a change. I did some research on why people think about suicide or try to commit suicide, and people have different reasons. At the end of the day, people don't want to commit suicide. They just want a change, a dramatic, drastic change in their life.

There was this therapist who wrote that it's okay to think about killing yourself, to imagine shooting yourself. It's okay to think about that, as long as you don't actually physically do it. Thinking about it is not unhealthy, it just means that there's something going on that needs to be addressed with therapists or psychiatrists.

When I became homeless, sometimes in my mind I would shoot myself over and over, depending on how bad the day was. Those kinds of thoughts made me feel a little bit better about it. To me, it's kind of like having a small, quick, kind of a reset, get me out of whatever I'm feeling, whatever I'm dealing with, giving me a little shake. Thought of it more like a reset button for me. That was a choice for me. It wasn't awful. It wasn't ideal.

How did you learn about the shelter?

When I ended up on a friend's couch, I started doing research online about homeless programs. There's a small office where people go to and say, "Hey, I'm homeless," and get help. Then a referral gets sent up to the homeless shelter, but until then, I stayed on a friend's couch for about a month and a half.

This was the summertime when they limit their beds. Basically, you have to check in with them every week. You have to go to the office once a week and you say, "Hey, here I am. Here's my current situation." Then they'll try to continue working with you and try to get you a bed at the Big House [Rockville, MD men's emergency shelter].

What was your impression of the shelter when you first got there?

It was big. It was big, open. Seemed very clean, organized. The bunk beds definitely reminded me of a boot camp because that's how the boot camps are. Bunk beds everywhere. I was told I could go to a shelter in D.C. before I ended up at the Big House. But I heard some really bad stories about the shelter in D.C. that there's no clean water, no showers and people doing drugs inside and people taking a shit in a bucket in the corner. I said, forget it. I'll just stay on my friend's couch. That was my initial impression.

I recall that a number of the guys in the shelter would come to you for advice or questions and you would advise and counsel them and help them find work. Do you remember that?

Yes, and I remember a lot of the guys came to me with their phone issues.

Their phone issues?

Right, because someone told someone that I was good with computers and good with phones. I would install apps on their phones so they could watch movies and TV shows. They would give me a couple of bucks here and there for doing it.

You, Will and I had talked about building some tiny houses in the county for homeless and low-income folks.

Right. We met with the developer and tried to partner up with them, but we ran into, if you remember, zoning issues and getting land leased in Montgomery County from the County government. That was the issue that the developer ran into. They couldn't get land to lease from Montgomery County.

But let's say we did build this program up. Let's say we got it running and we got the funding and land got leased, blah, blah, blah. Definitely there would have to be a screening process before you can accept the person because if you remember at the big shelter, especially in the winter time, you had people that were, well, interesting characters. One guy came in there one day, end of the day, drunk and pulled out a machete. Do you remember that?

I wasn't there that night, but I remember some other things.

Right. Of course the cops had to show up and he was banned from the shelter for that winter. I don't know if he was permanently banned, but once you pull out a weapon, that's it, you're gone. Doesn't matter if it's negative fifty degrees outside. You're gone.

Then we had this other guy, a real nice guy. He was an older guy in his sixties, maybe seventy, with a drinking problem. He would get sober for three days, get a haircut, shave and everything. Then he would be on a bender for two days, three days. Sometimes he would come in and the staff would know he's drunk and they'd just tell him like, "Dude, just go asleep," because he didn't cause trouble. He didn't fight with anyone, didn't argue with anyone. He just had a drinking problem.

Sometimes he'd walk around before going to bed while everyone's asleep and he'd take a piss on the wall because he couldn't make it to the bathroom or didn't know where the bathroom was because he's so drunk. Yeah, in order to run this type of program, you have to go through some type of a process of elimination to accept people who actually are working to get their lives together instead of just offering it to everyone which just brings in more issues, drugs, violence, any other type of crime possible that could destroy that community.

How were you able to get out of the shelter?

I was referred to transitional housing, the Dorothy Day Place. My counselor at the Big House sent a referral, then you set up an appointment and get an interview with them. Then they have to make a decision -- yes, we'll accept you into this program, or we cannot accept you for whatever reason.

For example, the guy with the machete, they're not going to accept him in there because of his past history. He will not be ever referred to that program.

In some states, there is no homeless programs or transitional housing at all. When COVID hit and people started losing their jobs, I'm looking on Reddit on the internet. People are asking, "Hey, I'm homeless. I don't know what to do. I don't know where to go," because some states and counties don't have anything because it's never been an issue.

My first advice was go find underground parking lots. If you're going to sleep somewhere in the car, find an underground parking lot. That's the first step. Then after that, contact your county officials, but at the end of the day, you might have to travel to another state if your county or state doesn't have homeless programs like we do.

Living in the car, that was actually an interesting experience. I found underground parking lots that were open 24/7. I think the worst part was just trying to sleep in the front seat. I think that's the most difficult part about it, living in a car. I had blankets and I had a pillow. A pillow made a huge difference, and a comforter in the winter. It's nothing like you'll ever experience. It gives you a completely different perspective about life. You get to see how people act and react when they find out you're homeless.

Then I got a basic membership at the Rockville Community Center. You get a basic membership, which is $45 a year and you have access to the computer room, access to the bathrooms and showers. You can come and go as you wish. Some days I would go to Panera Bread. I'd sit there all day and drink my cup of tea and have my bagel with cream cheese and tomatoes and nobody would care because I did not look like I was homeless. I was clean and shaven. I would do the laundry once a week or twice a week at the Laundromat. My spending was very little because I also had food stamps, so that helped out a lot.

At the same time, it's like a personal test too. It will test you being homeless, living in the car or a shelter. It will test every fiber of your being. At the Big House, it will test you psychologically. It will test you physically. It will test your immune system. At the Big House, I was sick. One winter I think I was sick five, six times.

I remember that.

I was in the ER maybe four or five times too. Being homeless, you get tested in every way. Your survival skills get tested. I'm trying to think of what doesn't get tested. I mean, your comfort zone, the bar of your comfort zone gets moved. Or it doesn't get moved. It just vanishes. Sometimes in the middle of the night, you have to find a place to take an emergency shit. Literally you have to run somewhere and just squat and take a dump. For me, it was not an issue because I grew up in the country as a kid, so taking a dump in the middle of the woods was no big deal. So I already had some survival skills.

What can we do as a society to try to end homelessness in this country?

We need to start learning from other countries, start learning from them, because some of them are pretty good at solving issues, all types of different issues -- medical issues, social issues, financial issues, homelessness. We need to learn from them, seriously, like first graders. We need to sit down with them and learn from them and apply their programs here in the states. But before we can do that, our government needs to change. Because as you know, our government is a circus. It's a shit show right now especially for the past year and a half. It's been a complete disaster and it's still ongoing. You can see it every day in the news.

Canada, for example, has its own issues with homeless people, but they have a program where they actually help people who have a severe drug addiction. They provide them with clean needles and a safe place to inject themselves with those drugs. We don't have that. It's not ideal, but at least it keeps a person alive.

We have to start changing. We have to change as a society to begin with. We have to change as a world to solve homelessness. We have to change as a world to solve so many different issues that we have globally.

Got a lot of work to do, don't we?

Yeah, as people, as human beings, we definitely have a lot of work to do. I don't know where I would even start to change it. It's like the program that you and I and Will tried to start. That could have changed something and helped out, but it's a start. It's a start.

Denis it was great seeing you, talking to you. Thanks for doing this interview. Let's plan to talk again. Take care of yourself.

You too.

MARLENE AIYEJINMI

Marlene Aiyejinmi is a survivor of homelessness, incarceration and addiction. She uses her experience to educate the public and advocate for the rights of people experiencing homelessness.

Marlene is currently attending Community College Preparatory Academy in Washington, D.C. where she has received several certificates. She is actively involved in her community and is represented as a public speaker by Community Family Life Services Speakers Bureau in Washington, D.C. Marlene's goal is to help others by sharing her life experiences with women who look to her for guidance, hope and inspiration.

Marlene, where are you? Are you in D.C.?

Yes, I'm in Washington, D.C. I live at Milestone Place. It's transitional housing funded by Community Family Life Services organization. I've been living here two years now, since I came back from being incarcerated.

Tell me about your background.

Talking about myself, how I became homeless -- I got married to a man from Africa who was never faithful. I drank a lot. I drank because I didn't have coping skills.

I got into some trouble and went to Lorton, Virginia Women's Prison. I got into a fight while I was intoxicated and cut a lady's face. I was sentenced to ten years, but got most of it suspended. I got released after ten months and then had eighteen months probation. I had no home. My husband had taken our baby and moved out of our apartment. And all of my things were just thrown out into the street. One of my sons -- his father had passed when he was three -- didn't have any photos of him. He was like, "You don't have a picture of my father?" All those things got thrown away.

Oh my.

Yeah. Everything! Pictures of my mom that they'd never seen before. And they'd ask, "Do you have any pictures of your mother?" I didn't have any of those things. They got thrown away while I was in prison.

I sunk into a very deep depression. I didn't know where to go. I went to my dad's home, which was not very good. He was an alcoholic. His lady friend was an alcoholic. I was in a bad place, a very bad place. I didn't know how to get out of it. I felt hopeless. I felt helpless. I felt like I didn't have anywhere to go. No direction.

When my dad lost his house due to taxes, I was on the street. I had one sister who at the time was living in public housing. She would drink with me. I got hooked on crack cocaine. As long as I could buy crack, I could stay in her house. But if I had no money and no crack, she put me out. She'd put me out in the middle of the night. It didn't matter if it was raining, if it was snowing or ice on the ground. No matter what.

This was in D.C.?

Washington, D.C., yes.

So from that point, I started trying to find women's shelters because I was diagnosed HIV positive in 1999. I didn't want to die. I knew I couldn't keep drinking. I knew I needed help, professional help. So I was told about a shelter called Open Doors for Women. So I went there. They had a nice shelter. You could come in, check in your bed at 7:00 p.m. and leave out at 7:00 a.m. So it was overnight. You kept your bed if you were there on time. But if you were late, your bed would go to the next person that was waiting for the next available bed. I missed my bed on several occasions due to my drinking, falling asleep somewhere.

They had a psychiatrist coming in from Unity Healthcare. His name was Dr. Robert Kingsley. He diagnosed me in 2002 as bipolar and depressed. And I could see that, I could get that, because I kept everything inside. I bottled up my feelings. I didn't talk about it. I was angry all the time. And they say when a person is drunk, their true feelings show up. Anybody and everybody that I was angry with, I cursed them out. I fought with them. I kept going in and out of jail and that would get me off the streets, a hundred twenty days, a hundred eighty days, depending on what my charge was.

Where did you go when you got out?

Every time I came out I had to go back to the shelter because I still didn't have a place to go. I still didn't have a job and needed mental health treatment. I still needed HIV treatment. I was sleeping outdoors at the church at 14th and Thomas Circle. Huge church there. And I would go up there when it got really cold. They would pass out these wool blankets. They gave you hot drinks at night, made sure you had gloves or ski hats, whatever they had to offer I took it. Every day I had to get off the church steps by a certain time. At 6:00 a.m. the maintenance man would come around and say, "Okay you guys, wake up, it's time to go." Go where?

Slowly but surely I was learning about places I could go just to get off the street. I would walk from 14th and Thomas Circle, Northwest, D.C. to 1st and O Street, Northwest, to a place called SOME's.

So Others Might Eat.

Yeah. I would go there and get breakfast. On certain days, I could get a change of clothing. I could take a shower. Someone said to me, "You should go the Rachael's Women Center." I'm like, "Well, what is that? And where is that?" Rachael's Women Center at the time was a day program for homeless women. They had case management there. You could get breakfast and lunch there. They opened from, I want to say 6:00 a.m. to 4:00 p.m. Monday through Saturday. Saturday they closed early.

Being on the street, I got robbed a lot. I got raped a lot. A lot of times I woke up and my medicines would be gone and my doctor was adamant about it: "We can't keep giving you medicine just for them to take it." The case manager at Rachael's Women's Center said she would keep my medicines in a pillbox in her office, which was a great help to me.

In the day program there was AA meetings. They took us on trips. They always taught us some type of skill, like parenting classes, learning how to take care of your children. They offered social services for people that were traumatized. I was traumatized, but not the way some women were. I mean, my husband never beat me. But what he did do was hurt me and scar me so bad emotionally that I kind of wish he would have just beat me more than hurt me the way he did. I felt like I was just a green card for him. And I believe I was.

You said he was from Africa?

Yes, Nigeria. From Lagos, Nigeria. I helped him get a green card. I had my first son with him. I was pregnant when we married, four months pregnant, and I found out he was cheating with a stripper. I went into early labor and had my baby at five months premature. He was a pound and a half. He didn't make it. His lungs weren't developed. On that very night my husband was with this stripper. At the time in 1990 they had pagers, beepers. They didn't really have cellphones. And I kept beeping him 911 because I was in the ER getting ready to have our first son, and he never responded.

After the baby died I said, "Okay, let's go ahead and get an annulment." We weren't married that long. I knew I couldn't live like that. I come from a dysfunctional family, my mom, my dad constantly fighting. She died at age forty-one from drinking. I saw history repeating itself in my mind. I had always said that I would never marry a person like my dad, then that's exactly what I did. The only difference was this man didn't drink. He kept a job. He kept a roof over our heads, but that's it. I got food stamps for my kids who weren't his. I got Social Security from my boy's father who had passed away from cancer. So I was getting a Social Security check and I was getting public assistance for my daughter, who has a different dad who was incarcerated.

All these things occurring at the same time was too much for me. I was twenty-five when I got married. Who would think that you would go through all that in your first year of marriage? I didn't think that. I mean, we dated for over a year. But they say when you date somebody, they treat you well when they first get to know you. And then after you say "I do," it changes. And it certainly did.

So he took our son while I was incarcerated in Lorton Women's Prison. My kids that weren't his ended up in the system. I did not know how to get them back, I had nowhere to take them. I found a shelter, at that time it was Capital City Inn on New York Avenue, Northeast. And your kids could come with you. The guardian ad litem for my sons and for me said, "Okay, you're in shelter now, we'll give your kids back to you. You should be able to get permanent housing with your kids either through Section 8 or public housing." That didn't turn out the way I wanted because Capital City Inn was infested with crack cocaine dealers and users, and the management had no control over that because they weren't there 24/7. Mostly all the women and mothers that were in shelter did receive food stamps and a check while they were in shelter waiting to get either Section 8 or public housing. The problem was that if you didn't use drugs, you either let the drug dealers in so that they could cut up and bag their drugs and give you a little money for using your room, or, if you were on the drugs, they would give you drugs for letting them come in your room and bag up their drugs. It just didn't work for me. I felt like I was falling even lower than before. I was just going deeper and deeper and deeper. Every month I would get my check and it would go to the drug dealers. Case management stepped back in and took my kids again.

At this point in time, I just gave up. I didn't care if I lived or died. My case manager was saying, "You need to get your act together. You're never going to get anything done because you're not trying to go to a program." A program was not going to make me stop. I have to want to stop on my own, and I didn't want to stop using drugs. It was the only thing at that point I thought that was giving me any joy.

What drugs were you taking?

Crack cocaine, marijuana and alcohol. I drank every day. As soon as the store opened, I was at the liquor store. Sometimes I would miss my bed because I would be so drunk I couldn't make it in. And I'd be sleeping on the street, which is how I would get robbed if I had any money.

I finally divorced my husband in 2012, which was the year of my last incarceration. The last charge was voluntary manslaughter. All of the past traumas and emotional scars, it put me in a bad space. It put me in a space that no matter what I did, I felt numb. I didn't feel sorry for myself. I didn't feel sorry for others. I didn't feel sorry for my kids. I just didn't give a damn about anybody. It didn't matter to me anymore. I had nothing to live for.

At that point in my life, if I would have died on the street, it would have just been one less person. It took me a long time to discover that I just needed to talk about it. Get therapy. Discuss what's going on with me emotionally and mentally. Not just keep taking the pills because I tried Antabuse to help me stop drinking. If I didn't take the pill, I could drink. But if I drank and took the pill, I would be very sick. So I knew if I was going to drink that day, I wouldn't take the Antabuse. And I would drink such large quantities. A few times I woke up in the hospital, in the ER, and they were saying, "Were you trying to kill yourself?" And I'd be like, "No, I'm not trying to kill myself. Why would you ask me that?" And they said, "Because of your alcohol level."

Alcohol poisoning. That happened a couple of times. And every time they put me in the mental ward. Kept me in there for a few days and I would come right back out and drink some more. I did try programs. I tried programs like WRAP programs. That didn't stop me. I went out and said, "Okay, I'm going to take just one hit and I'll go back in." In the meetings they teach you, one is too many and a thousand is never enough.

Tell me more about your children.

Finally, my kids are all grown up. One of my sons was going through some mental trauma himself because he had been in and out of the system so much. His dad was dead. My mom had died. He was my oldest son and she was in his life. So, him feeling like he didn't have anybody, he tended to act out. The other son, he emancipated out. He grew to be an adult, but he turned into a drug dealer. He never sold to me, but I knew he was selling it. By that time I was still drinking daily. In 2004, that son was shot and killed in Washington, D.C.

Oh no.

Yeah. They shot him at 21st and Maryland Avenue, Northeast. Then they drove his body to New York Avenue in a car and they left him there. The next day he was found by a security officer making rounds. Two weeks after that, the sister that constantly threw me out was killed in her apartment. Somebody went in and killed her. Like I said, she was an addict as well. And she's a cold case. It's still open, but it's a cold case. They couldn't pinpoint any one particular person because she had multiple people in and out of her apartment. And there were no cams. So with that being said, I now got two people dead in my family, my son and my only sister.

And my one brother, my only brother who was military, was just like, "Stop drinking!" He said, "I'm not going to drink anymore. You need to stop too." But how was I going to stop? I needed something to keep me numb. I didn't want to hurt anymore. And I didn't know how to cope with it. I went to the psychiatrist and told him, "Listen, I need you to give me something strong to help me sleep and relax, so that I don't keep drinking to the point where I'm blacking out." Because that's what I was doing on a daily basis, blacking out. I would see people and say stuff to people. I would fight people and have no recollection of it. I would see the same people the next day and they would say, "You don't remember what you said to me yesterday?" And I had no recollection of even being around them the day before.

Was the psychiatrist helpful?

Well I told him, "Listen, I see dead people." He said, "What do you mean? Like the movie Sixth Sense?" I said, "No sir, I see dead people every time I close my eyes." He said, "Why do you think you see dead people?" I said, "Because I keep going to the morgue to identify bodies. I keep going to funeral homes picking out caskets. I keep going to have family members dressed and they call to see if you like how they prepared your loved one to be shown to other family members." And every time I closed my eyes, I could vividly see my son on a stretcher. And I could see my sister. And all these scenes were like in my mind's eye like it was happening right in front of me.

I prayed. I went to church. I did all kinds of stuff. I asked God to help me because I believe in him. I believe in Jesus Christ. I just know that something was very broken in me and I couldn't fix it myself. The medicine wasn't going to fix it. Only God could fix it because he created me. And I knew things about drugs and what things led to what things, even to my HIV. Being promiscuous. Crack cocaine. Sleeping around. Not protecting myself. All that catered to my addiction. All that came from it. I wouldn't have been sleeping around if it wasn't for drugs. But at age fifty-one, I got my GED.

Congratulations!

Yeah, thank you. I never thought I would go back to school. I never thought I would accomplish anything. But prison gave me time to think and the ability to become completely sober.

Did you get your GED while in prison?

Yes I did.

You mentioned earlier that you were incarcerated for manslaughter. Can you tell me about it?

The day they arrested me I was drinking. The guy I was fighting with was a Hispanic male, Luis. He was a boyfriend that I was drinking with on a regular basis. He would come to the shelter at six o'clock in the morning with vodka in his backpack and forty ounce cans of Steel Reserve.

And like I said, I would blackout, and apparently I blacked out and I hit him too hard. His head hit on something and he bled internally. So that was in 2007. They didn't lock me up until 2010. I took a plea bargain. Something called an Alfred plea, which is not saying you're guilty or not guilty, because I knew I didn't want to hurt him. I cared about him. I was with the guy for five years.

So he was gone and I was here. I felt like I deserved to go to prison. The judge said he wished he could give me life imprisonment. But like I said before, the D.A. made a deal for eight to ten years, eight if I had good behavior. By then I had already served two years going back and forth to court, which was time served.

You said prison gave you time to think and the ability to become sober.

Correct. Right now I'm at eleven years sober.

Fantastic. Congratulations.

Yeah. I have a commendation from my probation officer for being compliant. I never had a dirty urine. I was supposed to have five years probation, supervised release. I got off papers in two years because I was compliant.

I'm fifty-seven years old as of last week. So I just want to live the best I can and help the people that I can along the way. Even with this book you're writing, I hope that it can let people know that just because you've been down, you're not out. Just because you've been an addict doesn't mean you can't get out. And prison actually saved my life.

Let's talk more about some of the programs you went through.

Like I said, I did every program. I went through the Step Down Program, which is a mental health program. I stayed in that for nine months. It gives you a stipend, like $40 every ninety days.

I did trauma programs and anger management programs three times because I went to three different prisons. I went from Danbury, Connecticut to Hazelton, West Virginia, ending up at Alderson Women's Camp in West Virginia, where Martha Stewart was at.

I did the RDAP program, which is for drugs. And it was a nine-month program. They would give you a year off your sentence if you graduated that program.

Did you get a year off?

No, I wasn't eligible. I had a manslaughter charge, but I still went through the program and graduated. I stayed in the program because I didn't want to get sent back out onto the compound where they were doing drugs.

Really?

Oh, absolutely. You could get drugs there.

Were you ever tempted to do drugs there?

Not at all. No, no, no. Since I got my head together, I became teachable. My mind was soaking up information like a sponge. I was clear-headed. I could see clearly. I could receive whatever I was taking in. I could speak. We had to write out and speak in RDAP weekly. For fifteen minutes you had to get up and talk about something that you did or you were doing. So me being in there for eighteen months, it helped me to open up more.

And then young ladies were coming to me saying, "Oh, Miss Marlene, you are so strong. Oh, I just love you and you're just doing so well. And I'm so proud of you. I hope I can make it through this." And I would say, "You can. You will. Just stay where you are. Stay focused. Focus on you. Focus on whatever it is you need to do to get you out of here and back to your kids and your family, whoever it is you want to get home too. Make it a positive move."

So where did you want to go back to?

I didn't want to go back to the old neighborhood where I was hanging out drinking. I didn't want to go back to a shelter. I wrote out a twenty-four month plan for myself before I was released from prison, and that included nine months in a halfway house. And I implemented that plan all the way through and I'm still doing it.

Good for you.

I know my story is like a lot of others and I'm not the only one. As part of the Speaker's Bureau, I tell my story because I want to be able to help people. I don't want people to look at me and feel sorry for me. I'm not that person anymore. They say what doesn't kill you makes you stronger. So I believe I could testify to that. I don't call myself strong, other people do. I just do the best I can, that's all I can do every day.

I saw you giving a speech on a YouTube channel. Very impressive.

Yeah, I'm a people person. I think I communicate well. I will tell anybody, anywhere, at any time that it's true what they say. Life is what you make it. It just doesn't come to you. Life isn't handed to you. You make it into what you want it to be.

Good advice.

I set a lot of goals for myself and I've met those goals. I'm still meeting those goals. It doesn't come overnight. None of it comes overnight. But you got to keep pushing. Motivate yourself. Put yourself out there, which is why I'm doing this interview with you. I want people to get it. Yeah, I used to be a bum on the street. I used to be out there dirty, stinking. I didn't have anywhere to take a shower. Hair nappy, cold, dirty. I was all those things.

Those things remind me that I don't want to be like that anymore. Now that I'm free of that, it's past. And my past doesn't define me. I got through that. I've adjusted to a new way of life, a better way of thinking. The people I'm surrounded with are positive people. Positive thinking people. And I'm in a good place. I'm in a very good place.

I'm so impressed and just in awe of your story. And I'm sure, especially among younger women that you talk to, you must have a tremendous impact on their lives.

I hope so. There was this young lady, about twenty years old, who was drinking every day. I said to her, "I'm trying to tell you, there's people out there that care about you. I'm one of those people. I care about you because I love you," and that's what I tell them.

"Even if you don't think anybody loves you, I love you. I'm telling you today, I love you." And that girl hugs me. She hugs me and says, "I love you Miss Marlene," and I said, "I love you too." Then she said, "You make me want to cry." "Why?" I asked. "Because you're just so nice."

I feel like my expression of love, it's not an act, it's not a facade. It's love that's always been inside, I just didn't know how to express it.

What does the future hold for you?

Oh man, I have seven grandkids -- four girls and three boys. And I have my first great-granddaughter, whose a year old. My daughter and my oldest son, we're very close, all of us. We do things together. I'm going to Busch Gardens this weekend with my daughter and her kids. We do a lot of traveling, things I had never done before. On my birthday, they took me to Rod 'N' Reel Resort at Chesapeake Beach. I had never played the slot machine in my life, but I played and I won some money. The food was good, the weather was great, it was an awesome day.

One of my grandkids is five and he's autistic. He's my favorite. I know you're not supposed to have favorite grandkids, but he's my favorite because to everyone else, he's way too energetic and standoffish, but not with me. He's a nana's boy. He loves his nana. When I go over there and spend a weekend, if I'm in the bedroom or on the couch, he comes and lays down beside me. I can be anywhere in the house, and he's coming. He got his blanket and he's coming. When I'm in the store, my daughter is trying to hold his hand, but he won't hold her hand, he'll grab my hand.

So the future means a lot of time with family. I FaceTime with my brother every other day. And I want to do more speaking engagements. I have a therapist that I can call any day of the week, even throughout the pandemic. And she talks to me for as long as I want to talk.

And I want my own apartment. I'm looking for my own apartment. I'm looking for a full-time job. I don't care if it's at Wal-Mart. It's $15 an hour. And if I have a steady paycheck, I can get my own car.

But my long-term goal is that within five to six years, I'm going to move to North Carolina where the majority of my family is. I've been in D.C. all my life but now I want a house in the country.

Well best of luck with all those future plans. Thank you so much for taking the time to talk with me. You're an impressive person, you really are.

Oh, thank you.

Take care Marlene.

I will. Thank you.

Bye now.

Bye.

WANDA STEPTOE

Wanda Steptoe is Executive Director of New Endeavors by Women located in Washington, D.C.

She has more than twenty years of experience working in various residential settings, including group homes for adolescents and adults with developmental disabilities, and has extensive experience in capacity building, supervision, quality assurance and compliance monitoring for federal, state, and accreditation standards and regulations.

Wanda also worked at Covenant House in Washington, where she established a crisis center and transitional living program for youth who were homeless.

She holds a degree in Special Education from Old Dominion University.

Good morning Wanda.

Good morning. Where are you calling from?

I'm in Cabin John, Maryland.

I'm familiar with that area. My first job was in Rockville at a place called Community Services for Autistic Adults and Children.

Yes, I remember reading that. It was a Spark Point interview.

Spark Point, I thought so.

Very nice interview. I read that you had a cousin who had Down Syndrome and that his doctors recommended that he be institutionalized, but his family decided to take care of him at home instead. You said that had a big impact on you and inspired you to devote your life to helping people less fortunate than yourself.

His name was Garnet. He was less than a year younger than me. He passed away in 2017.

I'm sorry.

My family was a very large family. My mom was the youngest of eleven kids, and I had thirty-five first cousins. Actually, Garnet's mother was my first cousin. As a very young girl, I recognized that there was something different about him, but he was raised just like the rest of us. He was held accountable for what he knew to be right and wrong. There was an expectation, and he had expectations just like we did. And he participated in the family, just like we did.

Obviously, his development was delayed, and as I got older, I realized that people like him were being put in institutions. But it makes a difference when you accept someone for who they are and provide them with love and you embrace them in a family. And also recognizing that there are different degrees of disability.

Some people may have medical issues that require a different level of care and all of that, but I think that his life, and growing up around him, I think it made me just who I am. I've always wanted to help people. I talk about him, and it's just a part of who I am. That's really the only way that I can answer that. And growing up in a very close-knit family, I think, probably had something to do with that.

Do you think you inherited any of that compassionate quality from your parents?

Oh yes. My mom was always very family oriented and my dad was the same way. He always wanted to help people, and even though it was just the three of us, he would cook like he was cooking for six people because he would give food away. So I think it just all had to do with how I was raised, what I saw.

What were some of your first experiences working with people who had experienced homelessness?

My first experience was working with Covenant House Washington. They serve youth who are experiencing homelessness. I opened their residential programs and it was like an aha moment. I felt like, "Why did it take me so long to realize this?"

They had what's called a "crisis center" for youth who were experiencing homelessness. And at that time, the residential program had ninety days to work with the youth to connect them with some sort of permanent housing, either reconnecting with family or whatever. A lot of the kids would drag their feet and not follow through on some of the things that their case managers wanted them to do. And in my mind, I'm thinking, "If I had ninety days to find somewhere to live, I would literally be busting my butt to do it." But I realized that what was normal for me was growing up in a home and not having to be concerned about where I was going to lay my head for the night. Couch surfing is what we called it, them going from place to place, because very few of them actually lived on the street, but they would stay here for one night, there for one night. So couch surfing was normal for them.

Having somewhere to stay for ninety days was like a luxury. It took me a while to realize that and to realize our different journeys. What's normal for us may not be what's normal for another person.

Then also we have generational homelessness. I don't know if people realize this, but if you grew up in a situation where you were couch surfing, or your parents didn't have a permanent place to live, that was normal for you. And if you become a part of a program, that's like a bonus. What we have to do, those of us who are providing services, is just like with your children. You provide experiences for them and try to show them a different way, try to help them establish goals and move beyond where they are. But some people are not going to move beyond where they are. That's why when people say end homelessness, that's not a reality.

Could you explain?

It's not ever going to be a reality as long as there is, for example, untreated mental illness, and that's also a reality of homelessness. To me, it's pretty obvious if you have people who refuse housing, and it's ten degrees outside, there's something that's not right in their thinking. Some people may not ever choose to leave homelessness, and it's sad, but it's a reality.

We try to help people see a different way, show them that you can live a different way. We can help provide housing for those who want it. I think a tangible way to end or to make a dent in homelessness is to reach the children in these families that are experiencing it.

Let's talk about the children. How does homelessness affect them?

We have a youth enrichment program, and I call that my baby, because it was my vision. And a lot of times, children who are experiencing homelessness have a tough time in school because of, number one, their parents may not know how to provide the support that they need to be successful. So in our family program, we have a teacher who works three evenings a week to help them. It's called the Youth Enrichment Program, YEP. It's part of the New Horizons program. The teacher provides tutoring, supervised homework assistance, extra help in math and reading, that kind of thing. A lot of times, kids don't like school because they're not successful. Our goal is to help kids be successful and understand what education can give them as they become adults.

That's really wonderful.

So that's one of the things that we do. As a consultant a long time ago, I worked with a program that served families and kids that were in foster care. I remember once there were two girls that I worked with. They had different fathers, but were raised by their mother, a single mom. And to make a long story short, this was a summertime program with a lot of enrichment activities. I remember taking them up to New York City. We took them on field trips to different museums, places in Maryland, places in D.C., and provided family therapy and other services.

One of these young ladies recently graduated with a Master's in Divinity from Howard. And the other one is what I call, and this is my term, "ghetto and satisfied." They both had the opportunity to experience that same program and to see these things, the same things. And one saw the bright lights of New York and said, "This is what I want. I'm out of where I was living. I want something different." And the other sister was just satisfied with that lifestyle. She's now a single mom. I think that taught me a lot. It's like, you provide people with opportunities to see something different, to experience something different, but ultimately, it's up to them what they decide to do.

Do you work mostly with women?

Yes. Our program is for women.

I've seen how homelessness affects men, or at least the men I worked with. It must be even more difficult and traumatic for women, especially women with children.

Yes, I think so. And especially those who find themselves homeless as a result of circumstances that are beyond their control, things like illness or loss of job, and you don't have family support, or you don't have a nest egg to fall back on. I think it is more traumatic for women because of that need to nurture and to take care of your kids. For women, it's more profound.

215

Is the experience of homelessness for women different today than it was years ago?

Yes. The needs of women have evolved over the years. Most of the women we served twenty and thirty years ago became homeless because of addiction or as a result of some type of catastrophic event that resulted in job loss. Now the women we serve have a plethora of challenges including trauma, lack of education and training, no employment history, mental health challenges as well as addiction and substance abuse. There are a lot of layers to work through and thus a longer period of time to become gainfully employed.

You said earlier that it's unrealistic to expect us to end homelessness because of certain personal circumstances such as mental illness. How can we slow it down?

I think a lot of it has to do with what you're doing, how you're helping people really understand homelessness, especially when you talk about women and the trauma associated with it. At times, I have found myself thinking about people who suffered trauma as children. I mean really traumatic things that no child should have to suffer. It's like, beyond these walls, nobody cares about your trauma. It's true, nobody. You still have to make a decision and take steps as to where you want to go and what you want to do. There's a lot of stigma associated with getting counseling, getting therapy. Some people will not get it. And so as a result of that, they kind of stay stuck.

Why won't they go?

It's a stigma and you have to face the trauma, facing what happened to you, talking about what happened.

And some people are not ready for that, because it's reliving it to some extent.

In the African American community especially, there's a stigma attached to it. Maybe it has to do with slavery because I maintain, and this is my personal opinion, that there's not too many things that are more traumatic than slavery and what our ancestors went through, being dehumanized, being beaten, having your children taken away, all of that.

And so we, as a people, overcame that, and so I think we're looked at as being or perceived as being strong. And so in the generations after that, there's this expectation that the strong survive, you know what I'm saying? You had to have determination. You had to be strong to overcome that.

I look at the African-American women I'm working with now. Yes, I recognize what you went through was traumatic. I can't imagine going through what you went through. However, you have to move forward. You have to take steps to move forward. Because again, beyond this agency, nobody cares about your trauma. When it comes to your landlord and paying your rent or being a homeowner, nobody cares about your trauma. They want their money. They want the job done.

I think sometimes we use trauma to make excuses, but at the same time, that can be to the detriment of the person because you allow them to remain stuck. And I'm not sitting here pretending to know what the answer is. I think that for each person, it may be somewhat different, but again, I think we need to recognize the trauma, but you also have to help people move beyond it.

How many women do you serve?

217

Usually around two hundred. The program is a transitional program, so we have up to two years to work with the women to find permanent housing, to take the next step. So it's transient. And then the other programs are permanent housing, so you don't have the time limit associated with how long they can stay.

Some people think that housing alone is the solution. All you have to do is provide housing and the problem is solved. It's not that simple, is it?

Absolutely not. Our newest program is for women fifty-five and older. I don't know if you're familiar with D.C., but when you're coming off the 295 in Southeast, there's a small park there. And you have people who hang out there all day. A large portion of them are homeless. When we started the transitional housing program, we had women who had been associated with that park. One of the women actually called herself Queen of the Park. The program has been in existence for three years, and these are literally women who've been homeless for decades. One of them had been homeless for thirty years. Some of the women experienced gang rapes. One of them would not sleep in her bed. It took us a while to get her to actually stay in the apartment versus going to the park and hanging out all day, because that's what she knew, that's all she knew. So it's a challenge and we provide support.

One of the things about New Endeavors by Women is that we have a phenomenal staff. We have staff that will go the extra mile to try to make a difference in the lives of the people that we serve. We had a person who was very afraid of going to the grocery store. The case manager worked with her and did a gradual thing to get her to actually go into a grocery store and shop.

I remember years ago I read an article in *The Post* about a man who had been living on the street. And when they got housing for him, he was sleeping on the floor. It took a very long time for him to sleep in the bed. And so putting people in housing and not providing support is not the answer. You have to provide support.

Apparently that's one area where we really need to educate people.

Right. There was this apartment complex in upper Northwest where they had moved some people in. The complex had upper-middle-class people living in it and then you started to have problems, like feces in stairwells and things like that. So that was an example of people just being dumped into these apartments and thinking everything is going to come up roses. No, you can't do what you don't know.

We also have to recognize the addiction issues. Addiction is huge and you can't just think that because you find housing, you're going to all of a sudden stop them from using. No, it doesn't work like that.

I know you're busy with the programs that you have. Do you have time to go into the community and educate people about what you're doing and about what the needs are?

Not as much as I would like. Sometimes I have the opportunity to talk to groups as a part of fund raising for the organization. But I'm more of a behind the scenes kind of person. I don't like talking in front of large groups of people. I do when I have to, but this type one-on-one with you, I am totally fine with. But large groups are not something that I gravitate towards.

What needs to happen to get people in government to pay more attention to homelessness and the needs of the homeless and to allocate more funding and more programs to help people?

I think it's education. It's really knowing what homelessness is all about, because even me, before I started working at Covenant House, I didn't know anything about homelessness. You look at people on the street and sometimes you think, "Why don't they just get a job?" It's a lack of knowledge. You can teach people things, but you can't teach someone to care. Unfortunately, there are a lot of people who just don't care.

Is there any way we can make it more of a political issue so that when people are running for office, whether it's the D.C. Council or Congress or whatever that we can make homelessness an issue? Any ideas?

In D.C., it's in front of your face on a daily basis. It's in front of your face. It's only when you have tourists or other people who get up in arms because they see somebody urinating in the street. That's when it becomes an issue. Or in my neighborhood, we've got these tents coming up. So I don't know. I can't even pretend to know what the answer is to that.

Talking about housing, are there ways to take abandoned buildings, whether they're apartment buildings or offices and convert them into temporary or permanent housing?

I think so. That would be good. HUD, for instance, does not like to fund transitional programs anymore. And I think that's a mistake because that's where you receive the most services. And again, this idea of just putting somebody in a house and everything comes up roses doesn't work. I think we need to go back to having more transitional housing where you can actually teach people life skills, the skills that they need to learn in order to manage a household.

I don't remember where they were, but I think it was somewhere in the Pacific Northwest where they were providing these little, basically like cubicles where people who were homeless could stay in.

Tiny houses.

Yeah. And so I think, again, you have to recognize that you have people who are not going to participate in a program and who are not going to come off the street. You need to help them go somewhere where they can have shelter and take a shower.

You have so many programs going on. You have New Transitions, Shelter Plus Care, New Horizons, New Hope, the YEP! Program, Rachael's House, New Journeys. How large a staff do you have?

Thirty-two. We have a total of seven programs and we do it with thirty-two people.

If you were to get a really large grant, what would you do with it?

I would invest more in the YEP! Program. I would do more transitional housing because again, I think that you have to teach people life skills. I would invest in more counseling services and recognize that you have to first build trust with people. And probably hire mental health therapists to help people gain trust and participate in counseling. Yeah, that's what I would do. I would invest more in transitional housing and teaching people life skills.

Prior to Housing First, in the transitional program when people gained employment, they were required to save thirty percent of that income. They got it back one hundred percent when they left the program. It was a means to number one, teach people about savings and the whole thought process so that when they leave and they get their own apartment or whatever, they have this little nest egg. Well now with Housing First, you cannot require people to do anything.

When you are getting something from someone, with rights come responsibilities. And I think it's a mistake that because you're homeless and because you've experienced this trauma, we're not going to quote-unquote, require you to do certain things.

So one of the things, if I had a whole lot of money that wasn't attached to federal dollars or local dollars, I would create programs that would have some requirements and responsibilities with it.

Where does your funding come from?

Primarily from the district and HUD. One of our objectives is to become less dependent on federal dollars, so we're trying to increase our individual donations as well as donations from corporations and foundations. But I would say eighty-five percent of our funding right now is government funded.

Some people don't think you should give a homeless panhandler any money because they think he or she will use it for drugs or alcohol. What do you say to those people?

You have people on the street that if you give them two dollars, they're going to use it for food. You have people on the street that will use it for something else. There was this guy on New York Avenue and I used to crack up because he had a sign that read, "I'm not going to lie, I want to drink." And people were giving him money.

When I'm walking the street and somebody approaches me, I offer to buy them food. You tell me you're hungry, I'll provide the food for you. I'll get you something to eat. I tend not to give money, but I offer to buy food. And so I think that we have to all do what we're led to do. I'm a believer that in general, if every person, wherever your passion lies, if you do something for that passion, the world will be a much better place.

You and I, as individuals, we can't reach everybody, but if we pursue helping those that we have passion for, it'll be a much better place to live.

I occasionally chat with a guy in Bethesda. His name is Tony. He's got one leg, uses a wheelchair and panhandles by the parking lot. Tony's been homeless for a long time. I'm trying to get him into a shelter but I haven't had any success. I'm building the trust as you recommended, but what do you say to a person like that? How can I get him to take that next step?

What's his objection to the shelter?

He was in a D.C. shelter and said it was terrible. People were defecating all over the place and fights and everything. He didn't want to go to any shelter. I told him that the Rockville shelter is different. You're going to get hot meals every day. It's clean. You got showers.

I think that you're doing the best that you can. If this shelter has an outreach team, maybe they could pick him up and bring him over just to see.

That's a good idea. I'll check into that. What other areas should we be talking about that I haven't thought to ask you about?

I can't think of anything.

The pandemic. I'm sure it's created havoc for you. How are you dealing with it?

We had two scenarios where we had people test positive for COVID. One thing I can say about D.C., I think that their response to COVID has been excellent. I think that the guidance they have provided has been excellent. So the mask requirement never stopped here.

The other thing is that D.C. has relationships with some hotels, because hotels were getting a lot of business when people were quarantined if they tested positive. The other thing was that we had people who didn't want to get vaccinated. So it's been a struggle, but again, we require the mask.

One of the things we did, for instance, was in our dining area where we can serve up to thirty people. We had tables that had seats for four at a single table. We took some of the tables out so that there would be fewer people at a time in the dining area. And so we had people eating in shifts. We did things like that to ensure everybody was properly distanced.

Everybody has individual rooms where they sleep. Outside of your room you had to have your mask on. I think that's the only reason we didn't have a large outbreak here because people have their individual rooms. But it's been challenging. The people we serve are no different than everybody else.

There were people we had to fight with to wear masks and others that willingly wore them and wanted to protect themselves and wanted to get vaccinated. There was just a lot of misinformation across the board. Politics aside, people know about the Tuskegee experiment and all of that, not trusting.

Anything else you'd like to talk about?

No. If I think of anything else, I'll shoot you an email.

Perfect. Feel free to do that.

It's been a joy talking to you.

Thank you Wanda. It was a pleasure meeting you and talking to you. I learned a lot and hope to be talking to you again soon.

My pleasure.

Take care.

You too. Bye-bye.

WILL GUNDLACH

Will Gundlach served in the U.S. Army Psychological Operations (PSYOP). The purpose and scope of these operations are to work in small, autonomous teams or with other Special Operations forces to persuade and influence foreign populations in support of U.S. military objectives.

While serving abroad, Will managed thousands of people, served as an airport director, oversaw the construction of schools, roads, bridges, canals and other major infrastructure projects, and created enablement training programs to help women improve their quality of life by developing basic household, medical, nutritional and business skills. On his return home, he experienced a period of homelessness.

Will holds a Bachelor's degree in political science from Washington College and studied cyber security at the University of Maryland. He speaks four languages.

Hey Will, how you? Still in the condo?

I am.

I enjoyed meeting your son. He seems like a fine young man.

He is, yeah. He's very compassionate, a great kid.

Were you an only child?

No, I wasn't, but I just didn't have the familial love there constantly.

Where were you born? Where'd you grow up?

I was born in Georgia and then lived in a number of different places. I lived in Florida with my grandparents for a period of time and then my sister and I lived in witness protection for a while during my mother's first divorce. We primarily grew up on the Eastern shore of Maryland where I would call home.

What was school like for you? Did you like it?

Yeah, I was afforded great opportunities. Both my sister and I were in Johns Hopkins gifted and talented programs at a very young age, in elementary school. Then we moved to the Eastern shore of Maryland and I believe it was at that time I took my SATs and had a near perfect score. Unfortunately, the family unit broke down for different reasons and then I ended up living with many different families.

So at that point, the community really took care of me. I was working after school, probably around the age of fifteen or sixteen. Had a job, had my own cell phone before adults even had cell phones and was renting an apartment and living on my own at this point.

What kind of jobs?

During the summer and weekends, I would work landscaping. I became an expert in landscaping, types of shrubs, plants, annuals, perennials, things of that nature. I was building Koi ponds on a professional level and I had a breadth and wealth of knowledge given to me in that employment.

Also, I worked as a sous-chef in one of the more prestigious restaurants. And that was great as well. It was a British couple that owned the place and they really took onto me. So I realized the opportunity I had at that point and thought this is a skillset that will just apply to my overall concept of who I'm going to be as a man. I definitely had a forward looking goal. It wasn't fully fleshed out, it wasn't polished, but at least it was in the right direction. I'm doing dishes, I'm cleaning, cooking at high levels. All of this was creating a standard and the quality that I wanted to be able to live and present myself and give to others that I care about in the future.

At that point you're still a teenager, right?

Right, and then I also did industrial roofing as well as construction during that period of time.

Not too many kids that age are doing that kind of work and that variety of work. How did it make you feel? Did you feel any different than other kids your age?

Yes, absolutely. I had more money than a lot of adults. And so I thought, well, I don't want to be doing this until I'm fifty, sixty years old and retiring. My body will break down and this just isn't conducive to what I believe is the goal of my life. And I knew I had more than that. I have an interest in art, I do oil pastels. Actually, let me get you one real quick. I got a really beautiful one too. I'm really happy with this one, Deno.

[Will shows his artwork.]

Beautiful!

I also worked taking care of terminal patients. This woman ran a halfway house for men who didn't have the financial assets. And so they lived in a small room and I would come and help Ms. Seal, who was a Dutch florist. And we would do flower arranging and I would help her.

Ms. Seal would make the food and I would carry the plates up to the men. And then we would play Scrabble, drink some coffee and then wash all the dishes for everybody. I always sought after grown men and mentors who had knowledge that I could trust and work for. I always looked for mentors who could increase my knowledge. I was patient to say, okay, this man has given me his time and his wisdom and his knowledge, and he's taken his time with me. And despite his faults, I'm going to accept that and take what I can from this person. And so I think that was a really critical aspect of accepting people for who they are and learning some type of tolerance, learning some type of forgiveness. These were well-respected men. These were men who were allowing me into their inner circle, into their personal life. The fact of the matter was that these men gave me time and allowed me to witness them in levels far above what I could achieve at that point in my life.

Did you feel that compensated for not having had a relationship with your father?

Yeah, absolutely. I mean, I did have issues. There were always questions of oh what if? Where would my daddy be to talk to me about this? Where would my daddy be of help? But at the same time, I find now with my own son, I don't always carry him through things. I let him fail, I let him get upset. I let him cry and I let him get it out. And then I say, hey, I'm glad you got your emotions going on, but let's identify them. Let's say, why are you upset? Let's look at this in a logical format and let's take the time, break it down just a bit. That's what I didn't have -- a man who was my father who would put a hand on my shoulder and say, it's okay, this is how you're overreacting to a situation or whatever, relax, calm down, I love you. And it's a very therapeutic thing for me to experience this with my son, because yeah, its like I'm healing myself.

What was happening after you graduated from high school?

I wanted to make sure that the family was sound. So even though I lived on my own, I was still very close to my mother, brother and sister. And that was important for me to make sure that they were safe, that they were okay. And when that was addressed, when my concerns were allayed at that point, I said, okay, I don't have opportunities here. This is not the life I want to live.

I was limited with what was available to me. And finance was a big thing for me. I knew that with the amount of income I had that I just wasn't going to be able to get there. And I said to myself, there's got to be something more. The military presented itself at some point and the U.S. Army is what I chose. And then I went straight into the Rangers, but before that, because my score was near perfect, they offered me something in psychological operations.

What does that mean?

It means to change, influence and persuade individuals, groups, entities, regions, persons, agencies, whatever, towards the benefit gains and objectives of the United States government, to see it as a palatable option. We end up calling the people the target audience. So it's a presentation of information in different formats or platforms to allow them to see options which can be more advantageous for their immediate position, which coincides with the goals and future objectives of the United States.

What was your training like and your first assignment?

They taught me foreign languages, several languages. I was exposed to many others by default, given that you're in something called DLI, Defense Language Institute. And I was chosen to speak Indonesian. So in a tight course of four months, I learned to speak Indonesian.

Did you find that you had a facility for languages? Did that come easy for you?

Yes, but honestly it has to do with a passion for it. You got to have the drive for learning this type of thing. You've got to be adept at it, but at the same time, you've got to have a love for it.

And so that was really something that I found to be the institutional format that I needed to justify things that I had been searching for in my life. Why did I latch on to this? I felt the need to become a well-rounded man with all these different skill sets to apply so that hopefully I could become the best father I could be, the husband and caretaker of my family and my house.

So tell me about your military experience.

When I went into psychological operations, I was studying the politics of Sukarno and Suharto, the Prime Minister and President of Indonesia, and learning why they made their choices. This was a huge moment for me to really go from a seed and blossom into a man. I had already prepared my body for the military experience. I was a strong country boy, you know me. I was constantly working. I was a hard man. Physically, what I was looking for was more. I would do the training and then I would go rock climbing and work out and swim on top of all that after work. And so, I was a monster. I was a machine. I was really going at it and I wanted that intensity. I jumped out of planes. I jumped out of helicopters. I was running around in the middle of the night with night vision goggles, and I did some pretty amazing things out there. I was interacting with the world and I was helping a lot of people.

Can you describe some of those interactions?

I started one of the first uniformed soccer teams in an incredible area in Afghanistan, near the border. And this was in 2001. This was the beginning of all of that. And so I found myself with an incredible opportunity to make analyses and assessments of local populations and people.

In an extremist Muslim population, these people were saying, wait a second, this guy is one of the most loyal, upstanding men we've ever come across. And he's not even twenty-five years old. This man is willing to bend over backwards and then some, and do somersaults to save us, protect us and help us. He's literally helping our village. He's literally helping our children.

At that point, I was operating nearly independent on the battlefield, which meant I could hop on a helicopter and go halfway across the country and do a mission with a whole different new set of people. So this type of action and mission was unheard of at that point in time. And especially for someone of my rank and my age. Some of my reports were going back to the White House during the Obama administration.

And so for me to realize that at such a young age, that my voice was literally carrying to the White House was just monumental. And I accepted and relished that responsibility and that obligation, and this to me was a blessing, regardless of the danger of the situation, to do all of these things in a whole new culture, to give them enlightenment and understanding. To tell them, hey, you can do your thing, live your life, but it doesn't have to be this way, and why don't you give me an opportunity to show you something else? That's all I'm asking and don't kill me in the process.

And after your military service?

So after this, I came back and I went into school for a period of time at Washington College and I built houses for a while. But I was very disenchanted. I just really got lost sitting in these classes with other students, going from high level negotiations with foreign officials overseas to this.

You had seen and experienced things that they would never see in their lives. Did you feel separated or apart from your fellow classmates because of your experiences?

Yes, but I tried to just put things aside and put them in a box. I really gave an effort to say, you know what, I'm going to do this fresh. I got to pay my dues do it this way, because maybe I'm not giving myself an opportunity to experience this type of evolution or increase of experience and knowledge. So I gave it the best that I had but that turned into a negative downward spiral where I did not feel I was achieving what I wanted. I couldn't escape the knowledge of what was happening out there in the world, knowing that every day that went by, my talents were being wasted, sitting here.

I just really had a strong calling and love for my fellow man around the world, and guess what, they came and found me and I went back overseas for about three or four years and lived in Afghanistan by myself for long periods of time. And that was under extreme duress and crisis and things of that nature. But this was everything that I wanted, so even though I gave up my ability to do the college thing at that point, I went halfway around the world. The chains and the leash were taken off. I could do what I needed to do, where the constraints of the bureaucracy, the politics, the military were not there.

Could you describe what you did during that time?

I ran the third largest airport in Afghanistan. I lived in Kandahar, one of the most dangerous provinces at that point in time. I've had my trucks blown up. I've seen my people killed. I've faced some very terrifying things, but at the same time, I was able to take my

236

program management experience and bring it to people with good-willed intentions. This was our United States American taxpayer dollars which were providing these people some type of stability, providing women the ability to learn, grow, take care of their families and homes, and then further help them and the economy by increasing the quality of life and livelihood of the surrounding area, their neighborhoods and businesses. And that was for women in an extremist Islamic population.

I was able to stay alive and my budget was $150 million. I had twenty-seven projects in total running. I think it was upwards of sixty thousand employees working and it was incredible. The landmass I was in charge of was half the state of Virginia to give you an example. And I'm flying from point A to point B to point C back and forth every couple of weeks. And so it was really, truly an awe-inspiring type of experience. I had the only civilian plane flying around southern Afghanistan at the age of twenty-six. That's bonkers. My counterparts were in their mid-40s and to this day, I don't know why I was blessed to have that experience, but I did. And I'm so grateful for that opportunity and I wouldn't have had it in any other way.

And you said that lasted for three to four years, and then you're back in the states.

Yes, then I came back to the United States, started looking for work, ended up working at Trader Joe's and immediately just hit the ground running. I didn't want to stop. I went from warlord level to literally cleaning bathrooms and stocking shelves in the grocery store, and I was okay with that and stayed fairly humble given my position and responsibilities overseas, where I was operating multinational operations.

So then it was like, okay, what am I going to do? Where do I need to be at by the age of thirty? And so at that point, it was like, I need a job, I need income and I need to go to school. I needed to take advantage of my GI 9/11 bill and make this happen. So I went into cyber security and I was doing fine. I had a relationship, wound up living with that girl, the mother of my son, and I felt that was socially appropriate and expected. We had like-mindedness to have a family and so on and so forth. But even though I had more experience in a genre of life that most people could never grasp, I came back to my country of origin, so to say, and I didn't know what I was doing. I was completely lost. The only thing I knew to do was to go to college and finish my degree.

Then there was a fire in our condo building. The fire trucks came and shut down the elevators. I carried a neighbor down fourteen flights of stairs. Another neighbor, an elderly Asian woman, died in the fire. My pregnant girlfriend went to her parents' house, and at that moment, I became homeless.

I was working full-time. I had a brand-new son. I'm working on a cyber security degree at University of Maryland. I had all this energy and I was making it happen, but this setback really took me for a spin. I thought I could pull out of this, and in two or three months find a new place because I had a little bit of money saved up. And then it hit me. I had always paid with cash and I didn't have any credit record. Try to rent a place with no credit.

I didn't stop working. I would go to the laundromat early in the mornings, just go to the bathroom, clean myself and shave. And, God bless that man, Mr. Kim at the laundromat who opened up every day at seven o'clock in the morning. Oh my God, if he didn't exist, I would have been doomed, absolutely doomed.

You said you were homeless after the fire. Where were you sleeping?

In my car. This was pretty tough and dangerous sleeping in a car because the temperature can actually be worse because it acts like a refrigerator. And so if you don't have moving air through there, you can actually freeze. And then you'll wake up with ice crystals on yourself. I wore two pairs of socks, pants, sweatshirt and sweater, winter jacket, hoodie, sleeping bag. The winter really does a number on you.

And then you'd have to wake up at a certain time, just to get out of there so that none of the residents that lived in the area would see you. So it took a lot just to maintain and keep working full-time and then it really hurt because you would go to these apartment complexes and they'd say, "Sorry, you have no credit." It just dumbfounded me though. I was like, are you kidding me? If you look at my history, there has never been a delinquent this or that. I've never borrowed money. I never knew that borrowing money was a good thing. But I was still working, paying child support and living in my car.

After my car broke down, I was literally done. There was no other place to hide. There was nothing else I could do. And the one thing was, I would not go to a homeless shelter. That was a huge thing for me, because I was out there helping while I was destitute and in crisis. I was helping people on the street. I was helping the men who were begging. I was buying extra warm, thick socks from the military surplus place and giving them to these older men who were staying near the Metro station. One of them died, sleeping on a stairway. I said, "You guys can't sleep here. The wind is flowing through this area and you're going to freeze to death, you just can't do it." And there were women out there that I was helping. I'd give them some food, this and that.

And so, it was interesting because people knew of me. They knew there was this man. They never knew that I was working during the day. This was like 2015, 2016 when we had some pretty tough winters with like two or three inches of snow at a time. It was tough, it was really tough. And it was dangerous for a lot of people.

How did you finally make the decision to go to the shelter?

Well there was this man, Officer Murphy with the Montgomery County Police Department. I talked to him at a gas station and this was just before my car broke down and I told him I was in the military and this and that. He told me to go to a homeless shelter that was literally right around the block where we were in Rockville.

When I got there, I didn't know what was going on. I didn't know what to expect. They gave me a warm cup of coffee and God knows I love coffee. That was nice.

I didn't talk to anybody for about two or three days, just to get a feel for the place. Really didn't know what to expect. I was on fine lines with custody of my son, so I didn't want to get into any fights or trouble.

Right.

Ultimately, things did seem to have promise. Things did start to go my way after a while. I just maintained who I was. Somewhere deep inside of all of this, there was hope somewhere. There was something that was moving forward. I could just feel it. There were men who were in worse situations than I was, and I was helping them.

Yeah, I remember that about you. Guys would come to you and ask for your advice and your opinion. I was so impressed with that. And then I learned the shelter was having you give speeches to people and groups in the community.

I think that was very cathartic. It was therapeutic in a way. I got to be someone of worth again. I had value. I got that from overseas and now in the most bizarre of ways, I was able to express it and utilize it and make it happen here. We went to the board of the County Council and different groups.

The Coalition allowed me to express myself and I saw an opportunity to help not only my individual case, but also all the other people at MCCH [Montgomery County Coalition for the Homeless]. I found that despite whatever challenges, impediments, situations, trials and tribulations people were facing, everybody really wanted to just progress and have peace and contentment in their lives.

The people at MCCH had genuine intentions to help. It wasn't a job. These people literally had their hearts and their passion in this work. I had relevant professional knowledge. I'd been on TV in other countries. I'd done large presentations. I spoke to large groups of people. I knew I could do this. I knew I could do it professionally and properly. And I knew that nobody else at the shelter could provide this type of perspective in this vernacular and achieve the same type of resonance throughout the community.

When we publish the book and go on the book tour, you're coming with me.

It's a deal.

Did your military training help you endure your homelessness?

Absolutely, because it would be a disservice to myself and everything that I went through. It would be a disservice to myself, to the men in my life who have mentored me, to the brothers and fellowship that I had overseas within the military construct. I mean, what a flop and a failure I would have been to just give up.

I want to be a father. I want to be a husband. I want to have a home and I want to love. That's not to say I'm not hurt from things that I've lived through because I do live with PTSD. I do have anxieties. I'm not perfect, but as God is my witness, I know exactly what I want and where I want to go and how I want to get there. I've never given up on that. Even though it felt like I failed, fallen flat, hit rock bottom, I still continued forward.

You're amazing, man.

Well, thank you, dude. Thank you.

You really are. I think you're going to impress and inspire people who read this.

Yeah, I hope so. I really want that. Everybody needs a second chance. Everybody needs forgiveness. Everybody needs understanding, compassion, patience. I believe that we should provide a little bit of time, a little bit of patience and understanding and really listen to what it is that individuals are being challenged with. We need to have the right strength, passion and intention to help people. We have to empower people as opposed to just dragging them along through life.

Thank you Will. It's been great talking with you. I look forward to seeing you in person soon.

Mc too. Take care.

Bye now.

Bye.

HEATHER THOMAS-WYCHE

Heather Thomas-Wyche is a community advocate and leader with experience planning, leading and improving business management functions in both business and social service fields.

She has extensive experience in providing case management services, risk reduction counseling, health education services and coordinating crisis interventions. Heather has experienced homelessness and is passionate about advocacy issues surrounding homelessness, food insecurity and mental health stigma.

Are you a Virginia native?

I'm a transplant. I came out here in 2008. My grandparents were living here. And I came with my four children, two who were adults. We came so we could be close to my grandparents, to help them out. Then they passed away a few years later, and we've been here ever since. But I'm from California. I grew up in El Centro and then moved to San Diego to finish my bachelor's.

What did you study?

Sociology with a minor in psyche. My first marriage didn't work out so I was a single parent going to school.

Did that course of study help you in your career?

Yes it did. In San Diego, I was in HIV and AIDS education and prevention field. So I did a lot of work in that field, wearing many different hats from volunteer to outreach worker, health educator, to eventually HIV test counselor, and then I was overseeing programs. So I got a lot of experience. I was part of the first legal needle exchange program in San Diego and part the first transitional housing program for homeless families. I was part of that when it first kick-started, so I've had a lot of really interesting experiences. Along the way I've seen good agencies and I've seen some really bad agencies. But even my negative experiences have had value because I've been able to learn, adapt and try to change things. I've now been in the social service and human service field since I was eighteen – more than twenty-five years at this point.

You said you've seen some good and bad agencies. Can you tell me the difference between a good and a bad agency?

I hate to say, but I think there's more bad agencies than good, to be honest. A good agency is going to be, first of all, very employee-centered. Because by doing so, they can better motivate their employees to be client-centered. And when you have an agency that does not treat its employees well, it's very hard for frontline staff and middle management to feel invested. And it's very hard for it not to trickle down in some capacity when working with the clients they serve, whether we're talking homelessness, substance abuse or mental health. So first and foremost, they need to be employee- centered.

They're also going to have the population that they're serving at the table in some capacity. Either they're going to have them involved or they're going to have some type of peer advisory board. They're going to involve their target population in some way, and usually a combination of both. They'll have folks working for them that have been through some tough situations. So they're engaging the current client population. They're targeting them in conversations, in focus groups, and letting them have a voice.

The agencies I've been at that I would consider to fall on the good side, you end up working not because you're being asked to, but you probably end up working twenty, thirty hours extra than what you're required because you want to, because you feel part of a team, you feel valued, you feel appreciated.

How do you determine the number of people experiencing homelessness across the country?

Have you heard of the PIT survey, the Point in Time Survey?

No

It's a survey that's done across the board nationally, where anybody who accesses certain types of services, like homeless shelters, transitional housing, those types of things which will be counted in the survey to try to get an idea of how many people are homeless in the area. How many are single? How many have families? The demographics, if you will.

But the problem is that it's not truly representative of what's going on out there. So for example, you and I could both be homeless. But if you don't go into the shelter the night they're actually doing the survey, even though everybody else knows that you're homeless in that shelter, you won't count as being homeless. On the other hand, if I go in and even if I'm only there for a few minutes to pick something up, I will count in that survey as being homeless. If they can't find somebody on that night, maybe the person went out of state, or went to visit someone, or they're in the hospital or what have you, they still won't count.

The other problem is, in that survey, they're not really looking at who's on the street, or in camp grounds, or somewhere else. There's different shades of homelessness. There's people couch surfing. So these people don't necessarily get counted in that survey. And for example, if you're homeless and you pay for a motel room, you're not considered homeless. But if somebody else pays for my motel room, I'm considered homeless. So there's all kinds of things and policies that give an inaccurate assessment of homelessness. And so, when thinking about changing it, we need to look at homelessness differently. We need to look at it through a different lens.

Did you know you wanted to get into this area when you were going to school?

I've always been an advocate. Ever since I was little, I've been an advocate. I've always stood up for social justice issues. I remember being eight or nine-years-old. Kids think about what they're going to be when they grow up. And I knew I wanted to work to end homelessness back then. I didn't know what capacity, because I didn't have any understanding of what that would mean, what that would look like, or anything. But I knew I wanted to end homelessness. I remember that was my dream as a little girl. So it's interesting when you look back that I really did gravitate to that mission in life.

You've devoted your life to the mission of ending homelessness, an experience you and your family went through. Can you describe that experience for me?

Here we were, my family and I back in around 2012. I'm working in social services in the homeless field. I had to step away from that work to help my husband with a small business he started and he needed my help. Fast forward a few years later through my twins pregnancy, health issues of my own, my grandmother's failing health, and all the responsibilities that come with that.

Well we lost our business and then became homeless. And so now I was on the other side of all that. For the first time in my life, I was having to access services like food stamps and Medicaid and homeless services that I had referred people to. I remember our journey started even before we lost everything, when we had to go over into Medicaid for the kids' insurance. And I remember going through that process of filling out the paperwork for Medicaid and turning it in. I had heard horror stories from clients that I worked with before. And so, here I go up to the Medicaid office, and I'm like, "Okay, here's my copy and here's your copy. Could you stamp my copy saying that you got it today, which shows clearly it's before the deadline that I have to turn in all of this documentation to see whether or not my children can get Medicaid? And they're like, "Okay," and they stamped it.

When I got home there was a letter in my mailbox saying we were denied because I didn't turn in the documentation on time, even though the documentation wasn't due until four days later. And I was like, "What the hell is this? Are you kidding me?" That was my first experience with what is going on with the system, and before that, working with my clients, I always tried to keep an open mind. Sometimes you do take some of the things your clients say with a grain of salt, because they're in crisis and there's a lot of stuff going on. But what my clients had said was obviously true.

Fast forward two years later, to when we lost everything, and it was like, "Oh, my goodness! What are we going to do?" And that's what people are dealing with, people who are homeless, or experiencing poverty, or food insecurity. And so I remember as we were going through the process, while I was pregnant with the girls, having to do all this pregnant. And then we became officially homeless after they were six months old. We were going through all this, knowing we were homeless and didn't know where we were going to go.

But thankfully, we were considered the fortunate homeless when we were going through it in the sense that even though we lost everything, we went straight from where we were into a transitional housing program. So we didn't have to stay in a shelter, we didn't have to stay in a motel, and we didn't have to stay in our car.

We're in Virginia, in Fairfax, Virginia no less. And we lost it all. But thankfully, because of my experience working in the field, and because I knew how to advocate, I knew where to look and what to do. We were able to get into a program. And even though I consider ourselves fortunate, it was the worst experience in the world. We were treated as though we were criminals. And that's the other thing that people who are homeless are battling against. What did you do to become homeless? What did you do that was wrong?

Could you elaborate on that?

In this country, being homeless, living in poverty or both, you are treated like a criminal. Homelessness and living in poverty have in many ways become criminalized.

I'm not sure I fully answered the impact of us being homeless had on our family and our kids. Our boys developed a lot of anxiety during this process. We all were treated differently by others. Our boys' education and learning have been impacted, as well as their health and our health. Their view of the world - they live in fear of having to move again. My husband is a combat veteran and he already had PTSD from his time in the military. This brought out his symptoms even more and has caused his health to decline. I think it messed with him the most. It messes with your self-esteem. Not to mention that our time in homelessness added to my own development of PTSD too. And as I mentioned, we were considered the fortunate homeless. It is much worse for others.

And that's what people are battling against, people who are homeless, or experiencing homelessness, or poverty, or food insecurity. And so we were going through this pregnancy knowing we were homeless, not knowing where we were going to go, where we were going to stay. We became invisible in a very broken system.

I was able to keep the kids in the same school and make sure we stayed with the same church group. But even now I am still learning the negative impact it's had on them. We had to move in that transitional housing program. We had to move four or five times in less than two years. That in and of itself is exhausting. You have to be constantly on guard when you're in those types of programs, whether it's permanent supportive housing, or transitional housing, or what have you. My case manager would reach out and say "They're doing an inspection," or "The landlord's doing an inspection" and you're in this constant state of anxiety. It trickles down to the kids. They feel that.

People treat you differently when they find out you're homeless. Just like systematic racism, it affects how other kids interact with your kids. It has been pretty traumatizing for these kiddos, my kiddos. They noticed a huge difference. "Why do we have to move again?" and "Why do we have to live this way?" It's exhausting. I put in a good sixty hours a week sometimes doing that, because you have to email this person, do this and that, make that call. And then there's the paperwork. But I think it's getting better. In certain areas, I would say it's getting better, because there has been a lot of research that's been done on ACEs, the Adverse Childhood Events and the impact it has on kids as they grow.

So that's one of the new buzz words out there - ACE. The other buzzword that's been out there is trauma informed therapy or trauma informed services, recognizing that everybody has some type of trauma that's going on that you may not even know about.

This kind of data coming out about different research studies about trauma and the need for trauma informed services, the need for early intervention services, and things like that, are really helpful and important.

You mentioned trauma therapy. Can you discuss how trauma affects people who are experiencing homelessness?

Trauma affects your mental and physical health. In my work through the years, I have seen people without any previous history of mental illness or substance abuse become homeless, and the longer they are homeless, the greater their chances are for developing mental illness, drug abuse and declining health, like diabetes and high blood pressure, and complications from these illnesses. And when you think about why that might be, well, being homeless, you live in survival mode and survival brain. It makes it hard to do anything in this state. It's traumatic. And the longer you live in survival mode, the more likely your brain chemistry is going to be impacted on a long-term basis. That could mean depression, anxiety, things like that. Humans are not meant to live in constant survival mode, fight or flight.

Being homeless, you are always at risk of being exploited, abused, raped, arrested, have your family separated or children taken. Being homeless, you have less access to quality affordable nutrition or quality healthcare, which over time has an impact on your physical health. I have had clients I worked with literally die because they were homeless for so long and the toll it took on their health.

Can you describe the federal government's housing choice voucher program?

In case you didn't know, when a person is awarded a HUD housing voucher, if they can't find a property that fits the criteria and a landlord willing to rent to them with a voucher, the same person or family can lose their voucher. What is wrong with this picture? Why are we not helping folks locate a place to use their voucher? Why is a person penalized if there are no viable housing options and they can't find a place to rent to them with the voucher? This policy speaks back to my earlier point about homelessness and poverty being criminalized.

Well what happens with those types of vouchers? You get into a situation where you're very fortunate if you get a good landlord, let's just put it that way, which I still don't understand, because it's really a good income for landlords to take on somebody with a voucher. You're given a certain amount of guarantee. You're going to get most, if not all of your money every month. You're going to get what you're asking for.

And with those vouchers, whether the transitional type of program like what we were in, or the Section 8, they get paid the month before. So January's rent from whoever's paying it for the voucher part, pays the landlord the previous month, in December for January. There's a lot of pros about it and a lot of education that needs to be done with potential landlords so that there can be more affordable housing stock options for people.

But in the transitional housing program, one of the places we moved into because we had a voucher, we were very much looked down upon by this landlord. And we knew the most we were going to be in it was a year, because that was all we were guaranteed as far as being in transitional housing. We didn't know anything beyond that. One of the first things she said when my husband and my kiddos got out of the car was, "I hope you can keep this place clean." And so we get into her place and this is where I can tell you how you're treated by some of these programs. Because there is such limited housing stock and because there's just a limited amount of landlords willing to rent to people with a voucher, the programs end up putting more value on that landlord relationship than on the people they're serving. And that's what happened to us.

I was searching day and night. I mean, nothing was coming up because you're given a certain amount of money and there are all these parameters. And so this was the only possibility I could find. I was reaching out to the housing locator saying, "Look, I've gone through the whole list," which by the way, housing locators, a lot of times send you outdated lists that they haven't taken the time to update. Or they're sending you lists, for example, with a three or four year waiting period.

I had a really weird feeling about this potential landlord. There were some red flags here that I just didn't feel comfortable with. I was really concerned about if we should enter into a lease with her. But there was nothing else. And it got to the point where you're like, "Well, are we on the street or do we just have to deal with her?" And so we entered into this and I went over to clean before the movers got there to move our stuff.

We knew the previous tenants had a dog, and I'm very much allergic to dogs. Thankfully they had hardwood floors through most of it, but they had carpet on the stairs and on the landings. The place was dirty. And so we're cleaning and my son gets bitten by something and gets all these bite marks all over him. I'm like, "Oh my goodness. What's going on?"

Long story short, it was fleas. So we went back and forth. We're like, "Hey, we think you might have an infestation." We took pictures and showed her. And we noticed every time he was on the carpet area, even though we had it steam cleaned, he would get bit. And she refused to look at the evidence. She called us filthy. She even tried to get the case manager to kick us out of the program and said all these horrible things about us.

My son was getting really sick. The landlord said "Well, you must have brought them in." So then she brought in somebody to do a bug inspection. He said we had bed bugs and all our stuff supposedly brought it in. I'm like, "But that makes no sense, because none of our stuff was in here when my son got bit." Thankfully, I had somebody that I was able to borrow money from to hire my own bug person to come in and do an inspection. He's like, "You have fleas is what you have. That's what's biting your son." So they did a report, we submitted it.

And we documented on the moving report issues with the hot water heater and issues with the HVAC. We went about ten days with no hot water in the middle of winter. I couldn't bathe any of my children. And if I took a shower, I had to do it quickly. Do you know how painful it is to take a cold shower like that in the middle of winter? It's like knives going into your body. So no hot water. And she wouldn't believe me that there was an issue until the water heater burst.

And then it flooded the basement. I'm like, "Are we concerned about mold? I'm a little concerned here." No, she didn't want to address that. So we dealt with that. Then the basement I noticed was flooding. I was like, "Hey, water's leaked in from outside. I don't want this to turn into mold." I'm doing my due diligence like you're supposed to, but she did not believe me about that. She wouldn't come out and look at it, nothing. So I took paper towels, stepped on them with my feet, took pictures, "Do you believe me now that this is wet?" So we dealt with that, we dealt with bugs. She finally went ahead and got the area treated. We dealt with no hot water. We dealt with the HVAC going out, her not believing us about that, all during this time period. And always treated badly and with the attitude of, "Well, you're fortunate to be here. Just deal with it."

Well I thought maybe we just got a bad landlord because there's bad apples in every bunch. But the more I talked to other people, and then even in my work with clients, I was like, no, this is a mentality going on among a lot of the landlords. They won't come in and fix stuff unless it's inspected and reported, which means they may not get paid.

I learned a lot about landlords during that whole process. But the housing agency that had our voucher refused to support us in any of that, because they placed more value on their relationship with the landlord than they did with us. That one year was one of the most stressful times of our life. And it's those types of things, that's the norm. As a person living in poverty, or dealing with food insecurity, or homelessness, or all of the above, you encounter that a lot.

So what needs to happen to improve the system that helps people who are experiencing homelessness?

You need good agencies. You need empathy. You're in the field of helping people, that's your job, and it's not sympathy. Sympathy means pity. It's about empathy, true empathy. You need to do a lot of education about what this means and why people end up homeless. You need better programs and better policies where people who are going through it or have been through it are at the table to let you know what's working and what's not working.

And then there's another characteristic I found going through it ourselves. And that's to learn how to advocate for yourself. That's important.

We also need to remember if the goal is to end homelessness, then we must make sure we have good after care programs and supports. A lot of programs are designed to end services as soon as a person or family moves into more stable housing. How many of those individuals and families re-enter homelessness again down the road? I have seen it more times than I can count. This is true even for those placed in permanent supportive housing programs. I have a family I am working with now that has been in the same PSH program for over five years but as soon as the agency placed her into their PSH program, they stopped most supports and check-ins within six months. This family sought me out as an advocate because of my previous reputation on treating clients with compassion, respect and dignity. After years in this PSH program, the program was trying to terminate her and her disabled son. I came in and started working with the family but it became very clear that I was doing the work as a volunteer that her own case worker, who was being paid, should have been doing. Having said that, I don't blame the worker. This goes back to something I mentioned earlier in our conversation - the importance of being an employee-centered agency. That worker was not in an employee-centered agency.

Is there anything else you'd like to share with me?

Well there's the issue of a living wage. There needs to be a legitimate living wage for people. Whether you work at McDonald's or wherever, there needs to be a living wage, because let's be honest for a minute, to say that people who are on a voucher are in affordable housing – that's not affordable housing. Or a tax credit property with a voucher – that's not affordable housing. If you're working a minimum wage job, then maybe most of your income is going for rent and housing expenses. Affordable housing is not having to need a subsidy. It needs to be truly affordable and that's a paradigm shift.

And finally, the definition of homelessness needs to be changed. We need to look at it more than just the person who shows up in one of those surveys.

Thank you Heather. Keep up the good work.

Thank you.

ACKNOWLEDGMENTS

We thank all of our interviewees for their participation in this book project. Hopefully, their stories, observations and recommendations will help educate the reader about the reality of homelessness and will encourage others to create more funding and programs to ultimately end homelessness in America.

Made in the USA
Middletown, DE
31 March 2022

63362152R00150